D1208020

STRUGGLE FOR GERMANY

STRUGGLE FOR GERMANY

by

RUSSELL HILL

LONDON
VICTOR GOLLANCZ LTD
1947

PRINTED IN GREAT BRITAIN BY RICHARD CLAY AND COMPANY, LTD.
BUNGAY SUFFOLK

FOREWORD

I SHOULD like to express my appreciation to those of my colleagues who have helped me with advice and suggestions for this book, as well as by an interchange of ideas in the many long evening discussions we have had in the course of my year in Germany (July, 1945 to June, 1946) as correspondent for the *New York Herald Tribune*. In these informal talks we all tried to arrive at a sensible interpretation of the day-to-day news developments in Germany and to fit these often perplexing events into "the big picture". The opinions and conclusions embodied in this book owe much to these discussions. I want particularly to mention the help of this nature I got from Kendall Foss, James O'Donnell, Toni Howard, Marguerite Higgins and John Scott, none of whom, however, bears any responsibility for the opinions here set down.

My particular thanks go to Kendall Foss for his suggestion that I use the device of what I have called "news pictures" to recall to the reader some of the background and colour of the events under discussion. These news pictures, which appear at the beginning of most of the chapters, are made up of extracts, sometimes merely short phrases, and headlines from my own despatches as they appeared in the *New York Herald Tribune*. In two instances I used extracts from documents that are basic to the material dealt with in the book.

I am deeply grateful to Joseph Barnes, to Catherine Phillips, and to my father, Frank Ernest Hill, for the suggestions they made after reading my manuscript. I should like to thank the *New York Herald Tribune* for granting me leave from my duties so that I could write this book in Berlin before returning home. I appreciate the co-operation I got from numerous military government officials in Berlin, and the helpfulness and hospitality that were shown me on my various trips into the American, British, Soviet and French zones of occupation in Germany.

New York, December, 1946.

5

CONTENTS

I

THE POTSDAM CONFLICT

News Picture

. . . *presidential plane had a fighter escort of twelve p. 47 thunderbolts all the way from brussels . . . will occupy three huge chairs at a round table ten feet in diameter and covered by a burgundy red cloth . . . russians have planted a twentyfour foot red star of geraniums pink roses and hydrangeas . . . the flags of the three allied nations will fly . . .*
STALIN LATE BIG THREE PARLEY DELAYED . . .

> 3000 *linen sheets* 30 *vacuum cleaners* 20 *lawn mowers* 100 *bedside lamps* 150 *bottles of button polish* 250 *bottle openers* 250 *corkscrews* 500 *ash trays* 25 *reams of writing paper* 100 *waste baskets* 20 *electric refrigerators and* 3000 *rolls of toilet paper*

. . . *GIs could be seen walking down the street openly with german girls . . . fresh fruit cold succulent melons and berries tomatoes and lettuce hearts rich linens and oldworld silver and fine glassware . . . special china from bavaria . . . gin and scotch and bourbon and vodka and moselle and rhine wines liqueurs from curacao to creme de menthe . . . one blackened roofless skeleton of a building after another . . .*

> *mr churchill arriving about ten minutes after the president had left could not deny himself the satisfaction of entering his erstwhile antagonists spacious but debrislittered private study and inspecting the underground bombproof labyrinth beneath the garden where der fuehrer is supposed to have lived his last hours*

. . . *trumans first meeting with stalin . . . germans had little difficulty in recognizing churchill . . . newspapers carried comment from pravda and moscow radio commentators . . . hope that germany will be ruled as one country . . .* NEWS BLACKOUT ON CONFERENCE NOW COMPLETE . . . TRUMAN SAYS US SEEKS NO PROFIT IN WAR . . . BERLINERS LOSE HOMES AS US TROOPS MOVE IN . . .

> "*there is not one piece of territory or one thing of a monetary nature that we want out of this war if we can put this tremendous machine of ours which has made this victory possible to work for peace we could look forward to the greatest age in the history of mankind*"

A 2

. . . the complete blackout on all real news about what is going on at the big three conference continued today . . . BERLINERS JAM SOVIET FILM OF CITY'S CAPTURE . . . US AND BRITAIN SEND FIRST FOOD TRAIN TO BERLIN . . . *nevertheless in the flooded railway tunnel connecting the anhalter and stettiner stations there are still a large number of corpses of germans who died in the battle of berlin . . . gave japan her last chance to accept allied terms of surrender or suffer devastation and destruction which would dwarf that meted out to germany . . . stopped to address 450 missourians . . .*

ZHUKOV ORDERS GERMAN PLANTS TO RESUME WORK . . . *boundaries reparations a unified policy toward germany . . .* RUSSIANS SAY HITLER MAY BE ALIVE BUT NOT IN ZONE THEY OCCUPY . . . *brisk trading began with the russians paying GIs* $500 *for a watch . . .* BIG THREE PARLEY IS EXPECTED TO END TODAY . . . *had to make longterm decisions which will determine the future of the next twenty years . . .* BIG THREE AGREE . . . *conference ended on a note of "great cordiality".* . . . *"renewed confidence that their governments and peoples together with the other united nations will insure the creation of a just and enduring peace."*

IN the last months and days of the Second World War the Nazi leaders fought on with only one hope left: that they would be saved by a conflict between their enemies. Adolf Hitler, believing his own slogan that Bolshevism was the enemy of mankind, was petulantly disappointed that the Governments of the western Allies did not act on his axiom. He failed to see that the very existence of his Nazi State provided the Allies with a basis for unity and a common goal, preventing the latent conflict between them from exploding.

The Fuehrer might have enjoyed a sadistic satisfaction could he have seen how quickly after the surrender of the German armies the struggle for power among the victors developed. This book will deal with that struggle as it has been waged in Germany itself, the homeland of the major defeated enemy. I may say at the outset that readers will be disappointed if they expect to see one side or the other blamed exclusively for the conflict that rages across the face of our uneasy world. There is no easy way of allotting responsibilities, and I reject the thesis that Russian unreasonableness is the cause of our troubles, just as I reject the argument that the United States was at fault for not adopting a conciliatory policy towards the Soviet Union.

There was a moment, after the guns had ceased to bark, when the peoples of the world may have hoped that the end of war would really mean the beginning of peace. Those of us who were in Germany could not long fail to see that this would not be so, as we watched four great nations begin the historically unprecedented attempt to rule and plan the future of a fifth.

These four victor nations represented opposed political and economic philosophies. There was the Soviet Union, a socialist State, self-styled a dictatorship of the proletariat. It was a country whose citizens and soldiers had been taught to distrust, fear and hate the capitalism of the West. They had a faith that their economic and social and political system was the right one, and the only right one.

There was Great Britain, with its tradition of world imperialism. Its representatives approached the job of ruling Germany almost as though they were preparing to establish a benevolent colonial administration in some backward area of Asia or Africa. That is only one aspect of the truth about the British. For their own country was turning from capitalism and imperialism to a democratic socialism. It was trying to find a way of planning its economic life without discarding cherished individual liberties.

There was the United States, still clinging to a capitalism the Russians scorned and the British could no longer afford. The Americans were relatively inexperienced in the job of administering a conquered people. Isolationist by habit, they were likewise inexperienced in international diplomacy and co-operation of the kind demanded by this German venture.

Each of these three nations was inclined to envisage a Germany reconstructed in its own image. The Russians saw the future Germany as a workers' State; the British as a social democracy; the Americans as a land of free enterprise. The fourth nation, France, was interested in Germany in a more negative way: the French did not care so much what Germany became as long as it remained weak and divided.

In international power relationships the economic differences between a United States trying to patch up an ailing capitalism and a British feeling its way towards socialism made little difference. The two countries were linked by common traditions, a common political philosophy, a common language and a widely though not universally held belief that they were dependent on each other for their national security. Nor did

Britain's start along the path to socialism bring it any closer to socialist Russia, which regarded the Labour Government in London with, if anything, even greater distrust than its Tory predecessor.

The Western and Eastern worlds were split more by fundamentally divergent conceptions about freedom and the rights of the individual than by differences in their economic systems. When the representatives of these two opposing philosophies came together to accept joint responsibility for ruling Germany, they had to decide on which system would prevail there. It was agreed that Germany was to be a democracy. That agreement was soon seen to be illusory because there was no common definition of democracy; and definitions are important in a world where words and phrases and slogans are given any meaning desired by the user.

To the Western nations democracy meant free elections, freedom of speech and religion, preservation of the traditional rights of man. To the Russians these were merely the forms of democracy, and to the idea of a "formal" democracy they opposed their conception of a "true" democracy wherein the workers or their representatives (who might be self-appointed) controlled the State. At one Four-Power meeting in Berlin, where this difference in interpretation became apparent, it was suggested that each of the delegates should give his definition of democracy. After listening to the definitions given by his three colleagues, the British member remarked that he could only reconcile these divergent conceptions of democracy by defining it as what four Powers could agree to inflict on a fifth!

It would be false to picture the conflict in terms of ideologies alone. The Western and Eastern ideologies corresponded to two world Power groups or security spheres. As soon as the ultimate defeat of Germany and Japan seemed inevitable, it had become apparent that the United States and the Soviet Union would emerge from the war as the world's two great, and only great, military Powers. Britain would retain a hold—a loosening hold at that—on its sprawling Empire, which would be indefensible against attack by a major Power without American help.

British post-war policy was developed with this premise as a point of departure, while American policy was based on the complementary premise that the security of the United States must depend on defence of the British Commonwealth and

12

Empire. A sizeable minority of public opinion in each country rejected these premises, and opposed the working alliance that was the fruit of these policies. It was held that such an alliance, even though it fell short of the formal linking of destinies proposed by Mr. Churchill, antagonized the Soviet Union, and made co-operation with that country impossible.

When the Nazi war machine folded up, the brave, tough, poorly equipped and often poorly clothed but very numerous warriors of the Red Army had occupied half of Europe. In many places they were within striking distance of points the British considered vital to the defence of the Empire, and particularly of its Mediterranean "lifeline".

These strategic points included Trieste, Salonica, the Dardanelles and the outpost line of the Middle East position: Turkey—Iraq—Iran. The Middle East stretches for thousands of miles of desert and mountain (with an occasional fertile spot like the Nile Delta) from Tripolitania across North Africa to the Arabian peninsula and north to Kurdistan. It is the bridge between three continents, and was considered by the British as the position that must be held for the defence of Africa and India against any attack from the north. In two wars they were barely able to defend it against the Germans, and they never lost sight of the possibility that they might one day have to defend it against the Russians.

The latter, in extending their influence and control through eastern and central and south-eastern Europe, could point with perfect logic to the necessity for securing positions that would protect their own frontiers. If the United States needed defensive outposts at Okinawa and Panama and on Iceland, why should not the Russians, too, be permitted to base the security of their country on a system of defence in depth? But in international politics statesmen do not take one another's professions of motives at face value. For all the Western leaders knew, the positions required by the Russians for defence might easily be used as springboards for attack. A thoughtful American might go back and read his Marx and Engels and Lenin, and see there set down that the class struggle was bound to be violent and bloody, and would end only with the complete victory of the workers of the world. He might then ask himself whether the men in the Kremlin still regarded the Soviet State as the bastion from which this war against the capitalist world was to be waged. If so, he would deduce that a new world war was in the offing, and would be unleashed as soon as the Russians considered themselves strong enough. The tactics of the Communist parties in the Western world might confirm these conclusions.

Yet the American could not be sure. Ever since the victory of Stalinism over Trotskyism in Russia there had been signs that the Soviet rulers were prepared to place the national interests of the Russian empire above those of the world proletariat. Were not the Communist parties in the West being used more as instruments of Russian foreign policy than as agents of the world revolution? Then the American must ask himself whether this nationalist Russian policy was expansionist, and if so, whether it had limited objectives, and what these objectives were. He must wonder whether their attainment involved Soviet domination over areas to which the Americans and British were not prepared to see it extend.

To the Russians, American motives seemed equally open to suspicion, American actions equally subject to sinister interpretation, American potentialities equally to be feared. The Russians were taught that the contradictions of capitalism inevitably led the rulers of capitalist countries to seek salvation in war. They remembered the armed intervention against Russia by the Allies, including the United States, after the First World War. They saw the United States extending its military bases thousands of miles beyond its frontiers. They saw America in exclusive possession of the atom bomb. They had no more grounds for believing in the purity of our motives than we had for trusting theirs.

In East and West the statesmen were thinking in terms of two worlds, and not in terms of the one world to which all those who supported the United Nations organization were supposedly committed. The hard fact was, nevertheless, that there was not yet one world. Realistic statesmen, in the West as well as in the East, could not afford to act as though there were one world until it had become a reality. We are still living in the age of power politics. The only thing that has been added is the terrifying element of the atom bomb. Until the nations devise an effective system of collective security (and until there is a world government there can be no complete security for any nation), they will continue to look to the old methods of guaranteeing their individual security.

In Europe the strategically most important area is Germany.

It is important first by its geographical location at the heart of the European continent, where the two worlds meet. If the Russians controlled Germany, they might well control western Europe. If the Americans and British controlled Germany, they would certainly increase their influence in eastern Europe (though the possibility was minimized by the amputation of East Prussia, Silesia and eastern Pomerania). Germany is important, too, because of its large, industrious population, and above all because of the coal and heavy industry of the Ruhr. This powerful war potential was exploited in two great wars of the twentieth century by German armies on the offensive.

The conquerors of Germany proclaimed that they must act together to prevent Germany from making use of this potential in a third war. Tacitly they recognized that they must also act to prevent it from being utilized by one Allied group against another. This was the greater danger.

It must be recognized that power relationships have changed fundamentally and irrevocably. There are only two great Powers in the world: the Soviet Union and the United States. These two are becoming stronger rather than weaker in relation to all other nations, including Germany. And they are the two greatest *European* Powers, even though they are regarded by the Europeans as aliens and outsiders.

The fear that the history of the last post-war period will repeat itself is based on a faulty appraisal of the present situation. After the first war, the United States, though potentially a great Power, did not act as such. It withdrew from Europe. Russia was temporarily eclipsed because it had been terribly weakened by war, revolution and civil war. In Russia, as in the United States, there were strong isolationist trends.

Now these two colossi are anything but isolationist. They are the chief protagonists in the drama of international politics. Germany, Britain, France are by comparison dwarfs in size, population, resources, industrial potential, and must play subsidiary rôles as the two giants battle for their respective ideologies. I believe that by and large Germans are more aware than Americans are of the secondary place Germany must take. Germany is about as played out as an aggressive force as France was at the end of the Napoleonic wars, and the more perceptive Germans are reconciled to this fact.

Thus Germany is mainly important as a position and as a possible instrument, not as a prime mover. In this circumscribed sense it is extremely important. It is also the place where Western and Eastern policies meet, clash and are tested. Berlin is not a capital: it is a forum, a debating ground, a fencing hall.

All this should be borne in mind in discussions of the disarmament of Germany, its denazification, its spiritual regeneration. The Allies agreed publicly that a disarmed, democratic Germany, a Germany that had neither the power nor the will to war, was to be fitted into the family of nations—the United Nations world. At the same time each Power was vigilant to see that if this end could not be achieved, it would not have been out-manœuvred, would not find itself faced with a united Germany, controlled by a possible enemy.

This statement is still an over-simplification, because amongst the three Western Allies there was no unanimity on the details of a German policy.

France demanded far harsher terms than any to which the United States and Britain were willing to agree. The French thought in terms of preventing the war they lost in 1940. France's security, in the French view, required that its German neighbour—a country with nearly twice France's population and far greater resources and industrial strength—should be kept permanently weaker than France. The Ruhr arsenal must be taken from Germany; German armies must never hold the spring-board of the Rhine bridges; the productive power of German factories must be destroyed. But even the French, when they talked about Germany, were thinking also of Russia, and of the day when the Germans might march into France with red stars on their caps.

The British, on the other hand, wanted a German economy that would provide the Germans with a tolerable standard of living and would permit them to contribute to the general European economy. They remembered what many others seemed to have forgotten, that wars have economic as well as political causes. Germany had been Europe's greatest market and greatest supplier; a Germany that ceased to export and import would depress the living standards of all European countries.

American policy hesitated between two possible courses. The first, commonly labelled "soft peace", at least by its opponents, stuck close to the British view. It was challenged by the "hard-peace" policy of the Morgenthau Plan, a detailed proposal to partition Germany, eliminate *all* of its heavy industry and withdraw American troops. The more extreme aspects of the Morgenthau Plan were never made a part of our German policy, yet they exerted a great influence, even after the opposite view was formally adopted (at the time of the Foreign Ministers' Conference in Paris, in July, 1946). The net effect was to introduce inconsistencies and contradictions into the American policy.

Each of the other nations had its own hard and soft peace school. In Britain the advocates of the former rallied around Lord Vansittart, a British Morgenthau. But this group had less influence on official British policy than Morgenthau and his followers had on American policy.

France, too, had its minority group. Its Socialist party was willing to compromise on the French demands for separation of the Ruhr and Rhineland, but was overridden from the right and left as the comparatively conservative M.R.P. and the Communists joined to vote it down.

In Russia, too, there seemed to be conflicting views about the policy to be adopted towards Germany. Naturally the conflict never came into the open, but it was implicit in statements about the folly of trying to destroy Germany on the one hand, and about the guilt and great reparations debt of the Germans on the other. Later it could be seen, too, in the implementation of policy, when efforts to rebuild the economy of the Soviet occupation zone would be succeeded by waves of reparations removals tending to defeat this purpose.

Every nation, in evolving its German policy, kept its eyes on the developing struggle for power between East and West as much as on the body of the prostrate enemy of yesterday.

These conflicting policies were still taking shape when the Big Three met at Potsdam to lay the foundations for peace in Europe. The document they produced was to become the charter of post-war Germany, the Bible of the occupation. Like the Bible, it is subject to varying interpretations. It is quoted in support of conflicting views, and its authority is cited in justification of the deeds and misdeeds of the occupying Powers. This is hardly surprising: the wording of the document is vague wherever the signatories were unable to agree but did not wish to appear to disagree.

For the sake of at least a surface unity, the settlement of fundamental issues was postponed. These included nothing

17

less than the future boundaries of Germany; control of the heavy industry of the Ruhr area; the total of reparations to be exacted from the Germans; the future political and economic complexion of Germany; and in general the severity of the terms to be imposed upon it.

One reason for the failure of the Big Three to handle these problems lay in the character of President Truman and in his peculiar position at that time. He was trying to make good as successor to Mr. Roosevelt, before United States and world public opinion. He hesitated to deviate from the Roosevelt policy, which in foreign affairs had been to subordinate everything to winning the war, to make whatever concessions to the Russians seemed necessary in the interests of harmony. The war with Germany was over at the time of Potsdam, but the war with Japan was not. Furthermore, Mr. Truman had little acquaintance with foreign affairs. And in all things he found it difficult to make decisions, to plan ahead, to develop a consistent policy, preferring to deal with each problem only when it confronted him or had practically overwhelmed him. For all these reasons the American delegation came to Potsdam at a psychological disadvantage. The British suffered under an almost equally heavy handicap, undergoing a change of government right in the middle of the conference.

The clue to Potsdam, as far as the Americans were concerned, was that it fell between two periods in American foreign policy. The war policy was being reconsidered; the post-war policy had not yet been developed. It is understandable that we should have failed to insist on a settlement of basic issues, leaving them instead to future negotiation.

Potsdam was the sequel to Yalta. Its stated purpose was "to carry out the Crimea declaration on Germany". At the Crimea Conference, held at Yalta in February, 1945, as the Allied armies were preparing their final onslaught on Germany from east and west, the Big Three declared:

> "It is our inflexible purpose to destroy German militarism and Nazism and to ensure that Germany will never again be able to disturb the peace of the world . . . It is not our purpose to destroy the people of Germany, but only when Nazism and militarism have been extirpated will there be hope for decent life for Germans and a place for them in the comity of nations."

These purposes were elaborated at Potsdam in such a way that they were made to seem particularly irreconcilable. The proposed amputations of territory and restrictions on Germany's industry and standard of living were so drastic that one could not help wondering whether they left any room for "hope for decent life for Germans". One could not be sure, because the new boundaries were not necessarily permanent and the amount of reparations to be required and of industries to be destroyed or removed was not fixed.

The Potsdam declaration announced:

"It is the intention of the Allies that the German people be given the opportunity to prepare for the eventual reconstruction of their life on a democratic and peaceful basis. If their own efforts are steadily directed to this end, it will be possible for them in due course to take their place among the free and peaceful peoples of the world."

Further, there was a kind of recognition in the Potsdam document that a balanced economy based on a tolerable standard of living was indispensable to the creation of a democratic Germany. The agreement stated:

"Allied controls shall be imposed upon the German economy but only to the extent necessary . . . to assure the production and maintenance of goods and services required to meet the needs of the occupying forces and displaced persons in Germany and essential to maintain in Germany average living standards not exceeding the average of standards of living of European countries. (European countries means all European countries excluding the United Kingdom and the Union of Socialist Republics.)"

This was one of the big quibbles of Potsdam. Taken literally the sentence means nothing. The Allies were not committing themselves to maintain in Germany a standard of living equal to the average of European countries. It was merely not to exceed that average. Presumably it could be considerably less. The Allies could leave Germany with no standard of living at all and still conform to the agreement. The question was: how could Allied controls assure the production and maintenance of any quantity of goods and services when it was not stated what that quantity was to be? The unfortunate Allied economists and generals who were given the task of implementing the above quotation from the Potsdam Bible by working out a level of industry plan were at a loss to know exactly how to interpret it.

They could have said : "Very well, we must leave the Germans with enough productive capacity to provide them with a standard of living high enough so that democracy will have a chance in Germany, and the Germans will not rally around the next demagogue who comes to them with a facile panacea for their troubles." That would have been a reasonable interpretation of Potsdam. But on another page of the Agreement it is said that "productive capacity not needed for permitted production shall be removed" and that "in organizing the German economy, primary emphasis shall be given to the development of agriculture and peaceful domestic industries".

Those charged with putting Potsdam into practice could have said : "Obviously this means that we must develop agriculture to the point where the Germans can live off their land. Otherwise they will need to import large quantities of food. In order to pay for these imports they will have to export the products of industry. But since we must remove a large part of the industry with which the Germans formerly produced their exports, this is obviously not the proper way to balance the German economy."

But then the Potsdam implementers would have come to the passage where it is said that all that part of Germany east of the Oder and Neisse rivers would be detached and placed under Polish administration. While the final boundaries were not to be fixed until the Peace Conference, it was obvious that these eastern territories could not be counted on in planning the German economy. It happened that they included, in addition to the mines and industries of Silesia, 25 per cent of Germany's arable land. Therefore Germany, which before the war produced no more than 83 per cent of its own food, must support an equal population (after the acceptance of millions of refugees) on 75 per cent as much land.

The Potsdam charter for a new Germany was no less vague about the important question of reparations. At Yalta the Big Three declared it is to be their "inflexible purpose" to "exact reparations in kind for the destruction wrought by the Germans". The Russians had proposed the figure of $20,000,000,000 to be split fifty-fifty between themselves and the other claimant nations. Officials of our State Department say the figure was accepted as a "basis for discussion" by the Americans (but never by the British).

At Potsdam the figure was brought up again. These same officials report that even Stalin then admitted it was higher than anything the Germans could be expected to meet in view of the large-scale destruction of their country, whose extent had by that time become apparent. But no other figure was agreed on, and the Potsdam Declaration stated merely:

> "Reparation claims of the U.S.S.R. shall be met by removals from the zone of Germany occupied by the U.S.S.R. and from appropriate German external assets . . . the reparations claims of the United States, the United Kingdom and other countries entitled to reparations shall be met from the western zones and from appropriate German external assets."

Russia was also to get 25 per cent of the capital equipment removed from the Western zones, as surplus to the German peace economy, and therefore available for reparations. For 15 per cent of the total, it would reimburse the Western Powers with stated raw materials and food, but would get the remaining 10 per cent free.

The reparations paragraph of the agreement gave the impression that reparations would be taken in the form of capital equipment and external assets only. This impression was reinforced by another paragraph which stated:

> "In working out the economic balance of Germany the necessary means must be provided to pay for imports approved by the Control Council in Germany. The proceeds of exports from current production and stock shall be available in the first place for payment for such exports."

Although this was the impression created, nowhere was it specifically stated that current production and stock would not be used for reparations. It later became obvious that the Russians were not guided by anything as vague as impressions, and that they interpreted the above provision as meaning that exports from current production and stock would be available for the payment of imports, *in the first place after they (the Russians) had taken what they wanted as reparations.*

It would have seemed reasonable that the Germans, however much they had sinned, and however great the amount they had to make good, should have been told exactly what was expected of them so that they would know that the harder they worked the sooner their debt would be paid off. It was certainly not reasonable to take away all capital equipment not needed for a minimum peace-time economy (whatever that minimum was to be), and then exact further reparations out of the production that had been defined as essential to that economic level.

This is what the Russians wanted to do and have been doing. There are two principal ways in which it is possible to go about taking reparations from a defeated country. One is to leave its productive capacity intact and take the reparations in the form of current produce. This method was tried after the First World War. It was even considered necessary or desirable at that time to lend Germany money with which to increase and modernize its factories. The loans were for the most part never repaid, with the result that the reparations collected were approximately cancelled out.

The second method is to reduce productive capacity, removing the "surplus" equipment as reparations. This has the advantage that the country's war potential is reduced, whereas by the former method it may be restored. From the point of view of efficiency in collecting reparations, the advantages of the second method are as hard to find as those of the first. The value of the equipment that can be removed cannot be equal to more than a fraction of the damage caused in a war like the last one. By the time the plants have been dismantled, transported and re-erected on new sites, they are almost certain to have deteriorated. Finally there is the danger that by these removals the balance of the country's economy will be upset to such an extent that the occupying Powers will have to contribute to its support.

Already the United States and Britain have been—to quote General Robertson, the British Military Governor—"paying reparations to Germany" in the form of food exports for which no return payment is possible. Although reparations removals are not responsible for this state of affairs, they might easily prolong it indefinitely beyond the period of dislocation that inevitably followed the end of hostilities.

By their exclusion of the French, the Big Three prepared further trouble for their subordinates who would have to implement Potsdam. One of the decisions of the Crimea Conference was to invite France to take a zone of occupation and a place on the Central Control Commission that was to rule Germany from Berlin. It would have been difficult not to extend this invitation, since France was as closely concerned with the German problem as any nation, and since a French army was at that very time in position to move into Germany alongside its American and British allies.

It is true that France was not a member of the European Advisory Commission when, in November, 1944, this body agreed on the control machinery for Germany and its division into occupation zones. However, on May 1, 1945, one week before V-E Day, the French ratified the agreement with no changes beyond those necessary to make it apply to quadripartite rather than tripartite government.

The agreement provided for a Control Council composed of the commanders-in-chief of the four occupation zones. Each member of the Council was to have a veto right. Since the French were offered joint responsibility in the government of Germany, and were given the right to veto any decision by the Control Council—its supreme governing body—they should certainly have been given a voice in drawing up the charter of principles upon which the government of Germany was to be based. But France was not invited to Potsdam. It never subscribed to the Potsdam Declaration. Instead, it reserved its right to accept those provisions of Potsdam which it liked and to reject and veto the others.

The consequences of this exclusion of the French became apparent almost immediately. In order to implement the Potsdam principle that Germany would be treated as an economic whole, the American, Soviet and British members of the Control Council proposed to proceed with the formation of the central German administrations provided for in the Declaration. The French member vetoed the proposal, refusing to consider any form of centralized administration for Germany until its western boundaries had been fixed. Potsdam had tentatively set the eastern frontier on the Oder–Neisse line. It had said nothing about the western boundary. The French wanted to detach the Ruhr and the Rhineland from Germany. The other three Powers neither opposed nor approved the proposal. It was an issue that should have been considered and settled at Potsdam.

Thus it can be seen that every time the Big Three ran up against a really big problem they were unable to reach agreement. There had been no real showdown, but rather a postponement of explosive issues. The handling of these was then passed on to subordinates, who were asked to agree where their superiors had failed. These subordinates—the generals and diplomats and their staffs of experts—now had to rule Germany while peace in Europe was still unmade. Their charter was the Potsdam (so-called) Agreement—an ambiguous and contradictory document.

II

THE RULERS AND THE VANQUISHED

News Picture

. . . *huge piles of rubble clutter the sidewalks and streets* . . . *german oberbuergermeister whom he took out of the buchenwald camp* . . . BRADLEY MEETS KONIEV BEHIND RUSSIAN LINES . . . *majority of the stores are closed* . . . *in a narrow alley in a badly bombed district the faces of women peer out of windows looking for customers* . . . *to general bradley was presented a fast bay riding horse from the don region and marshal koniev got a new jeep* . . . WEIMAR LOOKS TO FUTURE NONE TOO HOPEFULLY. . . .

> *"we the undersigned acting by authority of the german high command hereby surrender unconditionally to the supreme commander allied expeditionary forces and simultaneously to the soviet high command all forces on land sea and the air who are at this date under german control"*

. . . *recorded russian songs are played all day long as the interminable columns of uprooted humanity trudge slowly and wearily across back into russian occupied territory* . . . 68% OF BREMEN HOMES RUINED BY ALLIED BOMBS . . . *greater berlin will be divided into three parts* . . . LEIPZIG AWAITS RED OCCUPATION. . . .

> *"hereby assume authority with respect to germany including all powers possessed by the german government the high command and any state municipal or local government"*

. . . AMERICAN TROOPS ENTER BERLIN OCCUPATION ZONE . . . *ugly ruins of the kaiser wilhelm church grimly eyeing the dead avenue that stretches in a straight line in the distance.* . . . *as a tribute to general bradley marshall georgi k shukov had ordered his best troops to be present* . . . HITLERS MASSIVE CHANCELLERY RACKED BY WAR . . . *general assumption here that permission to speak with german civilians on the streets and associate with them in public will mean the end of non-fraternization* . . . *emphasized the "reasonable" attitude of the russians* . . . *greatest progress has been made in restoring the city subway* . . . *people are "living up to their agreements" he said and "playing their cards across the board"* . . . THOUSANDS FLEE GERMAN AREA CEDED TO POLAND . . . *question of the chairmanship of the*

25

*council was decided quickly and amicably . . . in one instance at least
the russians appear to have played their cards better than anyone else . . .*
CONTROL BOARD GIVES FRENCH BERLIN SECTOR . . . RUSSIAN STUDY
MADE EASY FOR GIS IN BERLIN. . . .

> *"control council whose decisions shall be unanimous will ensure
> appropriate uniformity of action by the commanders in chief in their
> respective zones of occupation and will reach agreed decisions on the
> chief questions affecting germany as a whole".*

WHEN the Big Three and their numerous staffs of diplomats
and military and economic experts moved into the Hohen-
zollern palaces on the tranquil Potsdam lakes and into the
nearby German Hollywood at Babelsberg, their generals were
already wrestling with the problem of establishing four-Power
government in Berlin. A secret agreement on the techniques to
be adopted had been in existence since the preceding fall.

This Agreement on Control Machinery for Germany was
adopted by the European Advisory Commission in November,
1944. It provided for a Control Council consisting of the three
commanders-in-chief, a Co-ordinating Committee (the three
deputy commanders) and a Control Staff, including a secre-
tariat, an administrative staff and twelve divisions or direct
rates. The limits of the zones of occupation in Germany were
also fixed at this time. The agreement was later revised to
include the French.

On June 5, 1945, the four commanders-in-chief met in Berlin
and announced to the world the principles on which the occupation would be run. The Allied Control Authority was in
effect to be the Government of Germany during "the period of
occupation following German surrender, when Germany is
carrying out the basic requirements of unconditional surrender". It was not stated how long this period would last but
merely that "arrangements for the subsequent period will be the
subject of a separate agreement".

Each of the commanders-in-chief held down three big jobs.
He commanded the occupation forces of his army, he was
responsible for military government in his country's zone of
occupation, and he was his Government's representative on the
Allied Control Council, charged with working out joint policies
for governing Germany as a whole. In the absence of unanimous agreement on such policies, each commander would
apply whatever policies he saw fit in his own zone. Eisenhower,

26

Zhukov, Montgomery, Koenig—these were the men upon whom these new responsibilities had been thrust. All four had won great reputations as generals during the war. This did not necessarily qualify them for their new functions. They had now to become administrators and diplomats as well as troop commanders.

There was a tendency, carried farthest in the case of the Americans and the British, for the commanders to delegate their authority in these matters to their deputies. Eisenhower and Montgomery knew or guessed that their assignment to Germany was temporary. They were content to let their deputies become the real military governors. Koenig gave the authority for military government to a civilian, Emile Laffon, an able young former leader of the resistance movement in France. Zhukov reserved more of the authority to himself, probably because under the Soviet system it is more difficult for subordinates to assume responsibility and make decisions.

There was a similar abdication of authority by the commanders of their diplomatic functions as members of the Control Council. Important decisions were increasingly taken, not by this body, but by the Co-ordinating Committee, composed of the four deputies. These men were generals, too, and were also to a considerable degree unprepared by experience and training to be administrators and statesmen-diplomats. It was a fortunate coincidence that three of them—Clay, Robertson and Sokolovsky—happened to be endowed by nature with many of the requisite qualities.

Clay is a man of strong personality and sharp intelligence, with an abnormal capacity for hard work. He likes to make quick decisions, and will make as many as possible without asking for instructions or guidance. He depends on his advisors more for information than for advice, and it is for this characteristic that he has been chiefly criticized, by subordinates who feel he takes insufficient account of their opinions. He is particularly expert at four-Power negotiation, and has frequently been successful in the rôle of mediator. As a Southerner (he is the son of a former United States senator from Georgia), he approaches the job of "reconstructing" a defeated nation with some sympathy.

The British General Robertson is a man with a keen mind, whose capacity for logical reasoning and lucid exposition is unsurpassed. Correspondents in Berlin enjoyed his Press conferences because of the way he had of conveying in precise, beautiful English the exact subtleties of intended meaning. He was a master of the art of answering embarrassing questions without seeming to turn them aside, but at the same time without committing any indiscretions. He was equally adept, in four-Power meetings, at stating the British view without giving offence to those who could not be expected to agree with it.

I do not know General Sokolovsky personally because the Russians are hard to approach and have not adopted the institution of the Press conference. All I can do is report that his colleagues respected his intelligence and abilities and found him more flexible in negotiation and easier to work with than most other Russians. The mutual esteem that grew up between Clay, Robertson and Sokolovsky was a helpful factor, though it could not of course overcome basic governmental disagreements. General Koeltz, the French member, was less outstanding than the others, and in any case his potentialities were strictly limited by his rigid instructions from his Government.

When these men took up their duties in Berlin in the summer of 1945 they had to deal with a country that was physically and morally prostrate. In Germany pre-atomic bombing had reached its highest development. By the primitive and laborious method of carting bombs that destroyed only the immediate areas of their impact, the British and American flyers achieved over a period of years an impressive totality of destruction. It required nearly 1,400,000 tons of explosives to accomplish the final result. Each of these tons represented about one bomber or escorting fighter flying several hundred miles from a base in England or France, completing its destructive mission and returning over those same hundreds of miles.

Not knowing about the impending atomic age which was spectacularly initiated at Hiroshima only three months after the old-fashioned bombs stopped falling on their own cities, the Germans thought they had taken quite a lot of punishment. The American soldiers who occupied one "beat-up" German city after another were inclined to share this opinion. In Berlin several tens of thousands of tons of bombs had been dropped by several tens of thousands of planes. The results were none the less gruesome for the awe-inspiring reflection that they were no worse than what could be perpetrated by a small flight of bombers carrying half a dozen atomic missiles.

I lived in Berlin during most of the period from July, 1945, to the autumn of 1946, and sometimes had occasion to entertain visitors who had flown directly from New York. In twenty-four hours they had been wafted from an undamaged thriving metropolis to a place where the totality of destruction is more overwhelming than in any other German city.

"This is more like the face of the moon than any city I had ever imagined," exclaimed Walter Millis, *New York Herald Tribune* editorial writer.

Joseph Barnes, our foreign editor, asked: "Why didn't any of you people tell us about this?", then conceded that it was impossible for anybody who had not seen it to visualize from a newspaper account what had happened in Berlin. Possibly readers had come to discount stories in which the words "flattened", "levelled", "pulverized", and "blasted" appeared with such monotonous regularity.

No city was literally flattened, of course. In Berlin a relatively small number of city blocks were completely levelled. Storms of fire had done the greatest damage. These had swept wide areas, and here blackened walls of houses and twisted steel skeletons of factories jutted up starkly amid barren heaps of crumbled brick and mortar. There was no district where one did not see individual houses partly or wholly wrecked by bombs. Great piles of rubble that had once blocked the thoroughfares now filled the sidewalks or gaps between the buildings. The total effect was grimmer than if the whole area had been actually levelled.

The Berliners lacked the facilities to clean up their city by tearing down the half-wrecked edifices, carting away rubble and repairing the less badly damaged houses, as the Londoners have done. The destruction was on too vast a scale. The city authorities estimated that there were nearly 1,000,000,000 cubic feet of rubble in Berlin, and they knew they had no means of carting it away. They would have to proceed laboriously to sift out this vast junk-heap, melting down the precious bits of metal, cleaning the bricks to be used again, salvaging planks for firewood. They discussed fantastic plans for dealing with the unusable residue: for instance, it might all be piled up in the Tiergarten, Berlin's Central Park (whose trees were already being chopped down to heat homes); this space could then be replanted to make an elevated garden.

Proverbial German ingenuity brought forth such inventions

as primitive brick-scraping machines and "rubble-utilization" machines. The cumbersome Teutonic name for these was *Truemmerverwertungsmaschinen*. For the most part the cleaning up—whatever could be done—had to be done by hand. Women who had been members of the Nazi party were put to work on it. Others volunteered, not from civic pride, and not for the 50 pfennigs an hour pittance they were paid (this was worth only 20 cents even at the pre-war exchange rate), but because manual labourers were placed in a higher food-ration category.

With the governmental, business and residential sections in the heart of Berlin knocked out, the city became decentralized. The occupation forces moved into villas in the outlying suburban districts. Berlin became a ring of small towns, circling a hollow core. The same thing happened in varying degrees in all the large German cities.

Over one ton of bombs was required to kill or wound one German in the pre-atomic age. The American air force has accepted 305,000 civilians killed and 780,000 wounded as the best estimate of German losses. (It is probably a conservative estimate.) About 3,600,000 dwelling units were counted as totally destroyed or heavily damaged, rendering 7,500,000 people homeless. Between 18,000,000 and 20,000,000 were deprived of essential services (gas, water, electricity) and over 5,000,000 were evacuated from bombed cities. Damage in forty-nine of the fifty largest cities in Germany ranged from "light" to "very heavy". Only one town—Halle on the Saale—had the good fortune to come out of the ordeal intact. A number of medium-sized towns, as, for instance, Heidelberg, Baden-Baden and Constance, were likewise practically untouched, and the small towns and villages outside areas where there was heavy fighting escaped destruction. The German countryside looks normal enough from the air except when one flies over a large city, and except for the relative lack of traffic on roads and rail lines.

It will be many, many years before Germany recovers from the blow suffered by its transportation system in the concluding months of the war. Allied fighter and fighter-bomber planes ranged at will over the enemy land, shooting up thousands and tens of thousands of locomotives, rail cars, motor trucks and barges. Under the best of conditions it would be at least a decade before the German economy could replace the lost material.

It is worth mentioning that the German war economy did not come to a standstill gradually as the result of years of bombing, but that it collapsed very suddenly in the last months of the war under the concentrated weight of bombs from the final air offensive. Before 1943 the much-publicized raids had practically no effect in limiting German war production, and in that year the total loss in armament output from air raids is put at no higher than from 3 to 5 per cent. The index of armament production actually kept rising throughout the war, and reached its highest point in the *third quarter of* 1944.

Of all the weight of bombs dropped on Germany by the United States Army Air Force and the Royal Air Force, 85 per cent fell after January 1, 1944, and 72 per cent after July 1, 1944. Thus, if the July 20, 1944, coup against Hitler had been successful, the Germans would have saved themselves the worst destruction to their cities. However, it may be plausibly argued that this destruction was necessary in order to bring home to the Germans the completeness of their defeat, and was therefore worth while. Unfortunately, it also cost several hundreds of thousands of Allied lives and an incalculable drain on the economies of all the Allied nations to teach this lesson to the Germans.

Until 1944 the German war economy showed an unexpected ability to recuperate from the effects of Allied raids. The example of Hamburg is instructive. During July and August of 1943, 8,600 tons of bombs were dropped on this city, totally destroying one-third of all its houses, and completely disrupting the normal processes of living. Yet within five months production had recovered to 80 per cent of normal. The explanation is that only a very small percentage of the buildings hit were military or industrial targets, and that even when a war factory was bombed, the proportion of damage to its vital machines was generally lower than of that to its buildings. This was because the Germans took special measures to protect the machines, such as building brick revetments around them. Aerial reconnaissance would report a factory in ruins, but in those ruins the machines might still be producing for Hitler.

Germany's productive capacity, greatly expanded during the war, was between 75 and 90 per cent intact at the time of the collapse, despite all the aerial offensive had done. Yet even if the armies had not overrun the country, the economy would have collapsed at about the time it did because the disruption of transportation had made it impossible for the Germans to continue moving coal, raw materials and semi-finished products to the factories and assembly plants. When the occupation began, the country lay prostrate, and the greatest efforts would have been required to bring its economy back to anything approaching normal. The moral as well as the physical reserves of Germany had been sapped by six years of war effort.

A similar phenomenon was noticeable in Allied countries. In France, liberation put people in a mood for celebration, but the end of the war was followed by a let-down characterized by an inability to make the strenuous efforts needed for reconstruction. The patience of the patient British was sorely tried when it became apparent that the end of the war meant not an easier life, but increased privations and as great, if less heroic, efforts. The Germans (despite a general fallacious belief to the contrary) had not been as fully mobilized or as closely rationed as the British until the last year of the war. But their sufferings from bombing had of course been greater, and they did not get the tonic of victory at the end. Nor could they look forward to a better life within the foreseeable future, so it is not surprising if the mood at the time the shooting stopped was one of apathy, listlessness and hopelessness. It is, indeed, a marvel that there was as much eagerness to begin cleaning up the general mess as there was.

In Berlin, for instance, the superficial progress during the first months was enormous. I say superficial because there was no great revival of production; but in other ways progress was made in the direction of a return, not to normal life, but to a kind of adjusted sub-normal life.

When the Allied commanders flew to Berlin on May 8, 1945, to accept the surrender of the German armed forces, the ruins of the city were still smouldering. Masses of rubble blocked the streets. Tubes, trams, buses, telephones had stopped functioning, and the inhabitants, cut off from contact with any part of the town beyond their immediate surroundings, were wandering about in bewildered search for food and water. Two months later, when the Western Allies returned to take over their occupation sectors, there was already a noticeable improvement. The worst of the rubble had been pushed aside. Food rationing had been instituted, if not regularized. Four daily newspapers were being printed.

By October 11 the tube network had been restored and its

trains were carrying more passengers than in 1939, although the city's population had been reduced by nearly a million and a half by evacuations. Shops were being repaired. In many buildings where the upper stories were completely useless the ground floor was renovated, and a fresh coat of paint and neatly lettered signs over the door proclaimed the reopening of a store. On the Kurfuerstendamm, Berlin's fashionable shopping street, art shops, book-stores, dress houses, cinemas, cabarets, cafés and restaurants blossomed in the ruins. By winter the cultural life of the capital was flourishing. There were the opera, the philharmonic, a score of legitimate stage shows and musicals, over a hundred movie theatres. A dozen daily newspapers achieved a combined circulation equal to the population of the city, and there were illustrated weeklies, humorous magazines and literary monthlies.

Yet during that same winter the people were chopping down the trees in the Tiergarten and the Grunewald, their favourite parks, so that they could keep warm in their draughty dwellings. They were journeying to the country to trade their possessions to the farmers for a few potatoes. The revival of Berlin life was largely artificial. It may have raised morale a bit, but it represented nothing tangible, it corresponded to no revival of production and commerce. There were dozens of dress houses and plenty of fashion shows, but there were no clothes. There were restaurants without food (except on ration cards), bars without drinks, stores without wares (except for stocks which were not being replaced). Most of the city's commerce was not in its stores, anyway. Whoever had anything worth selling disposed of it on the black market, or used it for barter.

Another fantastic aspect of Berlin life that gave it a dream or nightmare character was the price situation. To the average Berliner, the purchasing power of the mark was about what it was before the war, when the official rate was 40 cents to the dollar. He could still ride in the tube for 20 pfennigs, buy a newspaper for 15 pfennigs or obtain a rationed loaf of bread for 70 pfennigs. The worker or white-collar employee who earned 150 to 250 marks a month (wages as well as prices were pegged at pre-war levels) could pay his rent, buy the food to which his ration-card entitled him, ride in the municipal tubes and trams, buy his favourite newspaper and occasionally go to a movie.

He could not venture into the black market. Prices there

were so astronomically higher that one wondered whether the same currency was involved. The loaf of bread that cost 70 pfennigs at the baker's could be sold for 100 marks—nearly 150 times as much money. A pound of butter on the black market cost 500 marks. G.I.s sold cigarettes to the Germans for 1500 marks a carton and watches to the Russians for 5000 marks apiece. When they changed the marks at the military rate, they got $150 and $500 respectively—until the Army figured out that this bonanza was being financed by the U.S. Treasury, and currency control regulations were clamped down.

There were 3,000,000 people living in what was left of Berlin, and every thoughtful visitor to the city wondered what they were doing there and what they were going to do in the future. They could not exist indefinitely by "taking in each other's washing". Nor did there seem to be much point in having them kept on the dole either by the Allies or by the rest of Germany. Berlin had grown before the war to a population of 4,332,242 because in addition to its considerable industry it was the governmental, business and financial capital of a highly centralized State. But now its industry was crippled. The Russians had removed most of the machines from plants in the sectors to be occupied by the Western Powers. And in any case the Allies were planning to reduce the level of Germany's industry. Politically and economically Germany was to be decentralized, so Berlin, as the nerve-centre of the nation, would no longer be able to support the same population. It was doubtful whether it could even support its reduced population (the Allies forbade the return of evacuees except in exceptional instances).

Many critics have felt that it was wrong to make Berlin the capital at all. Some even said it was not worth rebuilding. "It would be cheaper to start from scratch on another site and leave the ruins here as an object lesson to the Germans," was a view frequently expressed, more than half seriously.

It would in fact have been more expensive to do this. The great cost of a city does not lie in its buildings alone. The streets, sidewalks, underground railways, sewers, water-pipes, gas mains, electric and telephone lines and the very foundations of the houses—everything on or below the surface—represent a very considerable investment; indeed a greater one than all that is above ground.

34

However, the serious objections to restoring Berlin as the capital of Germany were political. The French, and many Americans and Englishmen, argued that Berlin was the symbol of Prussian militarism, and that there was great danger that it would once again become the capital of a centralized Germany and the brain of future German aggression. Despite these arguments, the European Advisory Committee agreed in November, 1944, that the Control Council and any German ministries or central administrations would have their seat in Berlin, and that the Greater Berlin area would be jointly administered by the Allies. The Russians were anxious to keep the capital in their zone and use it to extend their influence from there throughout Germany. The Americans and British were glad to have a listening-post in eastern Germany and at the same time show the Germans that the Western allies took an interest in what went on in the East.

Since agreement on the techniques of governing Germany had been reached long before the end of the war, it would have been possible for the Control Council to move to Berlin and start functioning immediately after V-E day. The American and British staffs of experts were being kept "on ice", and could have proceeded at any time. But the Russians were in no hurry, and kept their Allies out of Berlin for nearly two months.

One can think of several probable motives for their action. First, they wanted time to complete their removals of machinery from the parts of Berlin that were to be occupied by the Americans, British and French. Secondly, they wished to organize the German administration of Berlin according to their own ideas and choose the personnel for this administration. Thirdly, they wanted to supervise the formation of national political parties and trades unions, hoping to be able to control the parties and unions in all Germany through their Berlin leaders.

When the British and Americans finally did enter Berlin, and joined with the Russians to form an Allied Kommandatura for governing the city, they agreed that laws passed and city officials appointed during the exclusively Russian period could be altered or dismissed only by a unanimous decision of the Kommandatura. Thus the Russians could veto any attempt to alter their arrangements or dismiss the people they had appointed (this did not apply to officials in the districts and sub-districts of the western sectors).

The Allies committed themselves to the principle of running Berlin along uniform lines, as one city rather than as separate zones. The sector boundaries were to be merely lines delimiting the occupation areas of the troops. Each nation would be responsible for local administration in its sector, but the city government would be run by the German Magistrate or City Council, under the direction of the Allied Kommandatura.

The first difficulties arose over the problem of feeding Berlin. The Western Allies felt that, as it was economically a part of the Russian zone, and normally drew most of its food from an area within a fifty-mile radius of the city, the Russian zone should contribute the major share of the city's food. This appeared all the more necessary as western Germany was incapable of supporting itself. However, the Russian view that each nation should contribute in proportion to the population of its sector prevailed. The food was put into a central pool and distributed by the Germans. Britain and America, unable to get enough for Berlin from the western zones of Germany, were forced to import food to meet their commitments.

Another point of friction arose when the Americans discovered that street, block and house leaders, appointed during the period of exclusive Russian rule, seemed to be terrorizing households. The Americans claimed that this system was "designed along Nazi lines" and that "numerous complaints received indicate clearly that a large percentage of the individuals comprising these groups are snoopers, strong-arm men and petty tyrants". The system was abolished in the American sector, and subsequently in the British and French sectors, but not in the Russian sector. It was the first instance in which lack of agreement between the Allies resulted in lack of uniformity in the principles upon which Berlin was being administered.

Meanwhile the Control Council was trying to get ahead with the job of ruling Germany in accordance with uniform principles. Its first regular meeting was held on July 30, while the Big Three Potsdam Conference was still in session. Eisenhower and Zhukov, Montgomery and Koenig were present. An American-prepared paper on the activation of control machinery was considered, and referred to the deputies to be re-drafted and submitted for final approval at the next meeting.

In the following weeks the control machinery was gradually

set in motion. This represented quite an achievement, since it was equivalent to forming a four-Power government. There were no precedents. Translating and interpreting added complications. Minutes had to be kept in three languages, and every time anyone spoke in a quadripartite meeting his remarks had to be translated twice. There were dozens of such meetings every month. The Control Council met three times a month, and the Co-ordinating Committee or the four deputy commanders met twice between each Control Council meeting. Then there were the meetings of the twelve directorates, most of which had sub-committees.

To see how the system worked in practice, one might suppose that the Control Council decided to draw up an export–import plan, based on the Potsdam Agreement. Its decision would be referred to the Co-ordinating Committee, which would send it on down to the Economics Directorate with an extract of the pertinent passage in the Potsdam Declaration. The Economics Directorate would pass the paper down to the experts on the exports and imports sub-committee for detailed study. This committee would do the spadework, but would probably find that while it could make certain technical recommendations, there were policy decisions involved, and these were beyond its competence. It might list the points on which there was lack of agreement, or it might prepare a majority and minority report. The paper would be sent back up to the Economics Directorate, and if no agreement were possible on that level, it would go on up to the Co-ordinating Committee. If there was still disagreement, it would come before the Control Council, and if the Control Council could not reach a unanimous decision, lack of agreement would be reported to the Governments.

The system had the virtue that unimportant matters were settled on the lower levels, while on important questions the areas of disagreement were narrowed so that the Co-ordinating Committee and Control Council could concentrate on basic policy issues. In practice most of the important decisions were made in the Co-ordinating Committee. If it could not agree, the difference was probably so basic that it could not be settled below the governmental level. The Co-ordinating Committee met six times a month, usually for several hours, while after the first couple of months the Control Council often had ten-minute meetings at which it did nothing but sign decrees and orders

37

already agreed by the deputies. Often several members of the Council would not even come to the meeting, but would let themselves be represented by their deputies. It even happened sometimes that all four would be absent, and that the four members of the Co-ordinating Committee would sit as the Control Council and ratify what they themselves had done, or refer papers back to themselves.

By the end of the first year the Berlin generals had agreed on most of the issues on which agreement was possible. Wherever their instructions from their Governments made it impossible for them to agree, they had reported back this lack of agreement—and waited. It became ever clearer that they would have to mark time until the Governments, through their Foreign Ministers, had agreed, or until they had conceded that they would never agree.

III
"THIS NAZI THING"
News Picture

. . . nazis here have gone underground and are determined to carry on the fight against american occupation . . . JACKSON DRAFTS US BRIEFS ON NAZI CRIMINALS SEES DELAY IN INTERNATIONAL TRIALS . . . *for twelve years they have been indoctrinated in nazi principles he explained . . .* RULE AGAINST FRATERNIZATION BREAKING DOWN POLICY CALLED DELETERIOUS . . . *not only the police but also the city administration is still riddled with nazis . . . first time in the history of warfare that an attempt has been made to treat a conquered people in such a way . . . military government is going ahead with the elimination of nazis but is proceeding cautiously . . .* 24 NAZIS INDICTED AS WAR CRIMINALS GOERING TOPS LIST DOENITZ SHACHT KRUPP RIBBENTROP LISTED IN 25,000 WORD CHARGE END OF NOVEMBER SET AS TRIAL DATE . . . PLOT AGAINST PEACE AND HUMANITY IS LAID TO CABINET ARMY GESTAPO.

. . . HITLER SUICIDE IS CONFIRMED IN BRITISH INQUIRY *. . . imagine the defense will consider it more fitting as i certainly should myself that they should be defended by german counsel rather than for instance by a member of the english bar . . .*

> *. . . everyone in the shelter or bunker received an issue of poison capsules on april 28 the inmates of the shelter learned with some mixture of incredulity and disgust of heinrich himmlers overtures to the allies through sweden by this time shells were falling around the shelter and on april 29 it was reported that russian tanks had broken into the potsdamer platz about 500 yards from the place where hitler was holding out in the afternoon of the same day hitler married eva braun the ceremony being performed by an official of the propaganda ministry in a small conference room in the shelter the newly married couple shook hands with everyone present and retired to their suite with hitlers secretary there they held a macabre wedding feast at which the chief topic of conversation was suicide one of hitlers last actions was to have his alsatian dog destroyed by april 30 the fighting around the chancellery had become desperate shells were falling continually near the entrance to the shelter der fuehrers last hour was described in the british report as follows at*

about 2.30 p.m. on april 30 though the exact time is uncertain orders were sent to the transport office requiring the immediate despatch to the bunker of 200 liters of petrol at about the same time hitler and eva braun made their last appearance alive they went round the bunker and shook hands with their immediate entourage and retired to their own apartments where they both committed suicide hitler by shooting himself apparently through the mouth and eva braun apparently by taking poison though she was supplied with a revolver after the suicide the bodies were taken into the garden just outside the bunker by goebbels bormann and one or two others hitler wrapped in a blanket presumably because the body was bloody the bodies were placed side by side in the garden about three yards from the emergency exit of the bunker and drenched with petrol because of the shelling the party withdrew under the shelter of the emergency exit and a petrolsoaked and lighted rag was thrown on the bodies which at once caught fire the party then stood to attention gave the hitler salute and retired . . .

. . . 30,000 PAY TRIBUTE TO VICTIMS OF NAZIS IN FIRST BERLIN RALLY . . . *russian prosecutor said i have the honor to present to the international military tribunal the russian text of the indictment against the main war criminals and fascist bandits . . . example of steadfastness given by the concentration camp prisoners should show every german man and woman that there is another heroism than that of the battlefield . . .*

. . . series of shots showing the charred body of paul joseph goebbels lying in the courtyard of the reich chancellery the spectators gasped when they saw the black but still recognizable face of the former propaganda minister it was a hideous caricature one blackened arm was bent upward as it had been frozen rigid by death every german there could not have failed to remember the expressive gestures of goebbels arms in life and the mobile distortions of his features now fixed in a distorted mask . . .

. . . CIANOS DIARY EVOKES INTEREST OF RIBBENTROP SCHACHT CALLED THE KEY MAN IN RISE OF HITLER . . . *well ribbentrop i asked him while we were walking in the garden what do you want the corridor or danzig not any longer and he fixed on me those cold musee grevin eyes of his we want war . . . that schacht favored the nazi war plans also was demonstrated by extracts from schachts own utterances . . .* INTERNED NAZI WOMEN FOUND UNREGENERATE . . . *would never have taken an order from goering because he was a fool in economics and i knew something about it at least when this passage was read in court goering threw his head back and laughed as though nothing schacht might say could*

touch him . . . there are eleven pregnant women in this camp said eddy
and the rest of them are frustrated as hell . . . US POLL FINDS GERMAN
YOUTH KEEP NAZI IDEAS . . . DENAZIFICATION MAY BE PUT IN
GERMAN HANDS.

THE late General Patton, whose military reputation, unfortunately for him and for everyone concerned, won him the top
military Government post in Bavaria, was quoted as telling an
impromptu Press conference that "this Nazi thing is just like a
Republican–Democratic election fight". The General thereby
showed that, like most Americans in Germany, he did not
understand what Nazism was.

Patton was one of several thousand Allied officials who were
supposed to give top priority to wiping out Nazism in Germany. There was nothing ambiguous about this assignment.
Roosevelt, Stalin and Churchill had announced to the world
from Yalta:

> "It is our inflexible purpose to destroy German militarism
> and Nazism. . . . We are determined to . . . bring all war
> criminals to justice and swift punishment . . . wipe out the
> Nazi party, Nazi laws, organizations and institutions; re-
> move all Nazi and militarist influences from public offices
> and from the cultural and economic life of the German
> people. . . ."

An ambitious programme. And it is a pleasure to be able to
report that the Allies were able to reach a considerable measure
of agreement on the punishment of war criminals and on
denazification policies and laws. Unfortunately there were
great differences in the way these policies were applied; and
denazification, like other basic problems, became a political
football, a grim plaything in the international struggle for
Germany.

Shortcomings in denazification on the part of the British and
Americans were depicted by the Russians as sabotage by alleged
sinister and powerful pro-Fascist groups in the Western
countries. Similar shortcomings of the Russians were pointed
at by publications in the West with such comments as:
"Naturally the Soviets use the Nazis; after all, Nazism and
Communism are really the same thing. It is only to be expected
that those fellows would get together."

Even the joint enterprise that was the Nuernberg trial ended on an international sour note. The Russian dissent (in my opinion quite justifiable) to the acquittal of Schacht, von Papen and Fritsche was used to cast doubt in the minds of the Germans on the motives of the other Allied judges.

In the case of the Americans, denazification suffered most, I am convinced, not because there was any sympathy for the Nazis in high places, but because few of our military government officers really understood what it was all about. In order to eliminate Nazism, you should know what it is. Before you can denazify Germans you should know how they became nazified. The average American just hadn't thought about this problem very much. He merely had an instinctive feeling that Nazism was bad.

Before I take up denazification (I know this is a preposterous linguistic fabrication, but I must use it for convenience), I believe it will be pertinent to examine some of the reasons why Nazism got such a hold on the German people, and how thoroughly the average German was converted to, or influenced by, this doctrine. I will also consider the extent to which the German people supported Hitler and his party, and the degree of responsibility and guilt that must attach to Germans as a whole and as individuals because of that support.

The war showed beyond a doubt that German soldiers fought hard for the Third Reich and that the civilian population gave it effective, if not enthusiastic, backing. There was very little sabotage of the war effort. Except during the very last months of the war, men drafted into the Wehrmacht fought on in situations where they might easily have deserted or surrendered if they had been so minded. When finally captured, many would say: "I am just a little man: what else could I do?" Others remained defiantly Nazi in their attitude.

I believe one can distinguish between convinced Nazis who kept a fanatical faith in Hitler, sharing all his ideas about racial superiority and the manifest destiny of Germany, and those who disliked many of the ideas and practices of Nazism but supported the war as a German war. They would argue that it is no crime to fight for one's country, and in this era of nationalism there are few people who would disagree with that principle. American soldiers would probably have greater respect for the Germans if more of them used this argument, instead of trying to convince the Allies that they would have opposed the Nazis if only they had been able.

There are few Germans who would not have accepted cheerfully the material benefits that would have been theirs if Hitler had won the war. Indeed, there were few who had any qualms about accepting the fruits of Germany's temporary victories—the indirect fruits in the form of loot sent back by soldiers from occupied countries. Just to keep the record straight, it must be added that Americans are in no position to be righteous about loot; the millions of dollars worth of goods looted by Americans and sent home with the co-operation of the Army authorities, not only from Germany but from liberated countries, places us on the same moral level as the Germans in this respect.

Another argument many Germans use in justifying their support of Hitler was that they did not believe he would get Germany into a war. If they mean by that that they thought he would succeed in getting the fruits of war without fighting for them, they are using a quibble. If they mean they were really deceived as to Hitler's aims and intentions, they are confessing to a rather extraordinary *naïveté*; they could of course plead the extenuating circumstance that they were no worse dupes than most of the rest of the world, including the leading statesmen of most of the Allied nations.

The truth, or one truth, is that the Nazi doctrine had a great appeal to certain elements of the German population and to certain prejudices, traditions and aspirations in all Germans. The Germans had learned to know the forms of democracy under the Weimar Republic, and even to some extent long before that, since parliaments with limited powers had been elected in Germany from 1848 on. But the ideas of freedom which have been a part of the heritage of Englishmen and Americans for centuries, and were spread on the European continent by the French Revolution, had not taken a very deep root in Germany. The Rights of Man had less appeal to the German mind than such concepts as power and discipline and order and economic security. In the example of the Western democracies and in his own experience with democracy the German believed he saw the proof that this security could not be attained under a democratic government. Even in revolt the German clung to order and discipline, as the development of German Marxism showed even before the National Socialist revolution or counter-revolution came along to provide a more compelling demonstration.

National Socialism had its greatest appeal to, and drew its

greatest support from, the German middle classes. To the millions of small shopkeepers Hitler offered relief from the competition of big business and monopoly capitalism. These he identified with "international Jewry", appealing to and stimulating the anti-Semitism of the petty bourgeoisie. Anti-Semitism in Germany was not deep-rooted and fanatical, as in Poland, but of that relatively mild type which is common in the United States. Most Germans would have been content to see the Jews eliminated as business competitors; their mass extermination was popular only with the lunatic fringe of sadistic gangsters who exist in any country (as witness the Lichfield trials), but who only in Germany were given a free hand to satisfy their perverted instincts.

To the disgruntled professional workers, doctors and lawyers and architects, clerks and salesmen and white-collar employees of all kinds, Hitler offered relief from the distress of the Great Depression. Caught by one of the worst of the recurring crises of capitalism, they were unwilling to turn to revolutionary Marxism for relief, and thought they found the answer to their troubles in the national revolution of the Nazis.

Hitler tried to be all things to all men. While appealing to the lower middle class through its jealousy of big business, he let the industrialists and financiers believe that this was merely window-dressing, and promised them relief from industrial strife through suppression of the labour unions. Without the help of these interests it is unlikely that he could have seized power: the financial aid of a Thyssen and a Krupp, the political support of a Schacht and a Papen, were invaluable in carrying the Nazi party through a critical period.

The upper class, the land-owning nobles or Junkers of eastern Prussia, who for two centuries had officered the Prussian armies, were won over by the extreme nationalism of the Nazis. They tended to regard Hitler and his gang as socially unacceptable *parvenus* who could be used to further their own ends. The parliamentary alliance with the German Nationalist party of Hugenberg gave Hitler the Reichstag majority he needed to seize and consolidate his power by constitutional means. The officer caste was keenly disappointed to find that it ended up by being controlled by Hitler instead of controlling him; but this does not lessen the value of the services it performed for him right up to the closing days of the war. The Junkers were recompensed by being allowed to keep their feudal estates—a reversal of Hitler's original programme for breaking them up which had won him considerable support from the semi-serf peasants of eastern Germany.

The Nazis were much less successful in winning over the working class. The pseudo-revolutionary aspects of the movement, its very name—National *Socialist* German *Workers* party —were designed to accomplish this. But the workers remained Marxist; they helped Hitler only indirectly, by the division in their own ranks. The Social Democrats and the Communists fought each other very often more bitterly than they fought the Nazis, and this circumstance contributed no little to Hitler's success. The workers of the large cities and the Catholic peasants of western and southern Germany, where there was a more equitable distribution of the land, were the only large groups that resisted the inroads of Nazism until its final victory.

A glance at successive election results in Weimar Germany will show statistically which economic groups were won over to Nazism. Traditionally each party in Germany represented the interests of a certain class or economic group.

The workers were Social Democrats, and this party had been the largest single one in Germany since 1890. However, it had been in opposition right up to 1918 because the middle-class parties invariably joined against it and their total strength was greater. With the outbreak of war in 1914 the Social Democratic party split over the issue of voting war credits, the minority group withholding its support from the Government's war programme. After the war this was no longer an issue, and the two groups merged again in 1922. Meanwhile in 1918 another radical minority had broken away from the party. The Communists took literally the Marxian doctrine of a violent class struggle culminating in a dictatorship of the proletariat; they also tied their strategy to Soviet foreign policy. The Social Democrats favoured attaining socialism through the techniques offered by parliamentary democracy, and, as their name suggests, they did not hold that socialism was incompatible with democracy.

The Democratic party was bourgeois-democratic, and left of centre; it represented mainly the interests of commerce and small business.

The Centre party was clerical and drew support from all Catholics, but in particular from the small, independent peasants of western and southern Germany.

The People's party, farther to the right, represented heavy industry, high finance and the more nationalistic elements of the intelligentsia.

The German Nationalists were the party of the Junkers, the nobility, the Army and the higher bureaucracy. This was the most conservative party, and sat on the extreme right in the Reichstag until the advent of the National Socialists.

The table on page 47 gives a picture of the relative strength of these parties from 1918 until the last election, in 1933.

The story told by this table is of how the Nazis captured the following of the mildly liberal and mildly conservative parties representing the various middle-class groups. The decline of the Democratic party and the People's party is particularly to be noted. Both lacked forceful programmes and forceful leadership after the murder of the Democratic party's Walther Rathenau in 1922 and the death of the People's party's Gustav Stresemann in 1929. The numerous small splinter parties of the centre, which built up a considerable combined strength in the 1920's, were reduced to complete insignificance as their voters deserted to the Nazis. The Nationalists lost less badly to the Hitler party, but were lined up on the side of the Nazis when the showdown came.

The large Social Democratic vote in 1919 was given in a revolutionary situation to a party that was then considered revolutionary. After participating in the responsibilities of government, the Social Democrats suffered as does any party in power when things are not going well. But if one takes the nearly 12,000,000 votes cast in the first Reichstag election for the Social Democrats and Communists as the basic working-class vote, it will be seen that it was maintained throughout, though it failed to increase in proportion to the growing electorate. As economic conditions worsened, the Social Democrats lost votes to the revolutionary Communists, who, like the Nazis, opposed the democratic principles of the Weimar Republic and would have substituted a dictatorship. Among the group of voters impatient with democracy, there was some shifting back and forth between the Communists and the National Socialists, with the latter winning out at the end.

The moderate parties tended to revive with improved economic conditions. This is seen, for example, in the change from the May to the December election of 1924. Stresemann's "Great Coalition" Cabinet, embracing all groups from his own

	Constitutional Assembly,* January 1, 1919.	1st Reichstag, June 6, 1920.	2nd Reichstag, May 4, 1924.	3rd Reichstag, December 7, 1924.	4th Reichstag, May 20, 1928.	5th Reichstag, September 14, 1930.	6th Reichstag, July 31, 1932.	7th Reichstag, November 11, 1932.	8th Reichstag, May 5, 1933.
Percentage of eligible voters voting	83·1	79·2	77·4	78·8	75·6	82·0	84·0	80·5	88·8
Nationalist-Socialist Party	—	—	1,918,310	906,946	810,127	6,379,672	13,765,781	11,737,010	17,277,180
German Nationalist Party	3,121,500	4,249,100	5,696,368	6,205,324	4,321,563	2,451,686	2,177,414	3,019,099	3,136,760
German Peoples Party	1,345,600	3,919,400	2,694,317	3,041,215	2,679,703	1,693,878	436,012	661,796	432,312
Centre Party (Catholic)	5,980,200	5,083,600	4,860,027	5,250,169	4,657,796	5,185,637	5,788,019	5,326,067	5,498,457
Democratic Party	5,641,800	2,333,700	1,655,049	1,917,765	1,479,374	1,205,521	371,799	336,551	334,242
Socialist Democratic Party	13,826,400	11,151,200	6,008,713	7,880,963	9,152,979	8,575,244	7,958,712	7,247,956	7,181,629
Maj.	11,509,200	6,104,400							
Min.	2,317,200	5,046,800							
Communist Party		589,500	3,693,139	2,708,345	3,264,793	4,590,160	5,282,626	5,980,102	4,848,058
Small Parties	484,800	869,800	2,754,263	2,365,080	4,326,912	4,268,673	1,126,991	1,102,409	634,693
Total	30,400,300	28,196,300	29,281,186	30,283,805	30,753,247	34,956,471	36,882,354*	35,471,745*	39,343,331

* Including about 1,000,000 votes from areas subsequently taken from Germany by the Versailles Treaty.

People's Party and left of it to include the Social Democrats, had stabilized the currency following the runaway inflation of 1923; had concluded the Dawes Agreement reducing reparations; had improved Germany's international relations, thereby making possible an influx of foreign credits and loans; and had ushered in a period of relative prosperity. As a consequence, the Nazi vote was more than halved, the Communists lost 1,000,000 votes, and the moderate parties all gained, including even the moribund Democratic party. Four years later, in 1928, the Nazis had lost still further, and the Communists had not gained much. The onset of the world depression changed all that; and in 1930 the Nazis suddenly rocketed into the position of Germany's second strongest party.

Two more years of economic crisis helped the extreme left far less than the extreme right, and in 1932 the Nazis doubled their vote again and became the largest single party in Germany. Their opponents failed to take advantage of their electoral setback later in that year, nor did they exploit a temporary split in the Nazi party. Despite President von Hindenburg's personal contempt for the lance-corporal, he was persuaded by the land-owning and heavy industry interests he represented to help Hitler to power.

With financial and political support from these vested interests, the Nazis were able to put on a successful electoral campaign. Their victory at the polls must be explained in terms not only of the votes they took from other parties, but of the previous non-voters they mobilized. They cut down the percentage of the electorate that was too indifferent to go to the polls, and their appeal to the nationalistic aspirations of the youth won for them a large percentage of those who were voting for the first time.

In the final election of 1933 the Social Democratic party and the Centre party were the only ones supporting the Weimar Constitution which were able to maintain their positions. Only 13,000,000 votes were cast for the Republic. Its avowed enemies, the Nazis, the Nationalists and the Communists, together got over 25,000,000 votes. This was the true measure of the German disillusionment with democracy. Two months later the Reichstag deputies of the Catholic Centre party joined in voting extraordinary powers to the Hitler Government; they thereby signed the death-warrant of the Republic as well as of their own party.

48

The development of German opinion in the next twelve years is impossible to describe statistically. Active opposition was ruthlessly put down wherever it appeared, and Germans who disagreed with the policy of the Government were silent about it if they were wise. From 1933 to 1945 about 800,000 German political dissidents passed through the Nazi concentration camps and prisons (according to figures provided by a Dutch officer, himself a concentration camp "alumnus", who subsequently made a study of the books of the camps and prisons).

The bulk of the population was inclined to accept the inevitable. There was little rejoicing when war began. The sensational victories of 1940 raised hopes that it would soon be over, and subsequent checks and defeats brought a corresponding disillusionment. The popularity of the Nazi regime oscillated with the successes and failures of German arms and diplomacy. It was eventually condemned in the minds of most Germans because it failed in its aims rather than because its aims were wrong. The attempted coup of July 20, 1944, was, in the minds of the majority of those participating, a sensible attempt to end a losing war before Germany should be ruined, rather than an effort to destroy a tyrannical government for its oppression of the people. Lack of decision and courage on the part of the conspirators combined with ill luck to wreck the plan.

Allied troops entering Germany were surprised to find that nobody was a Nazi any more. The Germans had deserted the lost cause. They were even inclined to accept the Americans and British as liberators. This did not go down very well, because the tenacity with which the Germans had fought was still fresh in the minds of the Allied soldiers; and nearly every day was bringing fresh news of gruesome, last-minute atrocities committed in the concentration camps by S.S. thugs. In those early days there was little inclination to distinguish between "good" and "bad" Germans. One week after V-E day, Mark S. Watson, the correspondent of the *Baltimore Sun*, wrote:

"One of the fears most frequently expressed by Americans deeply concerned with the need for prolonged discipline of the Germans as a people, rather than of war criminals only, has been that we would invent some method of distinguishing 'bad Germans' and 'good Germans'. The point of this anxiety was a firm belief that there is no such thing as a good

49

German among all of those who by their total silence these past fourteen years gave tacit approval to all German abominations.

"Assurance can be given that so far as any observable rules or procedures are concerned there is here no official classification of good and bad Germans.

"There is a classification of a sort. Perhaps it is describable as identifying 'bad Germans' and 'particularly bad Germans'. In the latter group inevitably are Nazi party men, Gestapo and Storm Troopers. In the other group is everyone else."

This report reflects the mood at the end of the war. It was a mood that could not last. For one thing, neither Americans nor Englishmen can sustain over a long period an anger and hate against an entire people. Then justice compelled them to admit that one reason for the Germans' "total silence these past fourteen years" was that those who did not willingly remain silent were forcibly silenced. Finally, and pragmatically most important, the occupation was based on the premise that there were "good Germans". If there were none, how was Germany to become a peace-loving democracy that could eventually take its place in the family of nations?

One must draw a distinction between the concepts of responsibility and corrigibility. To say that the German nation as a whole was responsible for Hitler and the war is not to say that the Germans as a race are incurably war-like, aggressive and "bad". The latter theory, which has gained considerable currency, smacks strongly of Nazi racism in reverse. The traditions of Prussianism are a part of the cultural heritage of Germans even beyond the borders of Prussia. It has left its mark on the thinking even of those who are sincerely anti-Nazi and anti-militarist. In an age of violent nationalisms, German nationalism has taken a form that is particularly violent, aggressive and intolerable to any non-German. Yet there is no reason to assume that the Germans cannot be cured of aggressive and arrogant Prussianism just as the French were cured of aggressive and arrogant Bonapartism.

It would not be an easy job under the best of conditions. I have already suggested that one difficulty is that the Allies do not agree what democracy is and what kind of democracy should be taught the Germans.

There were plenty of other difficulties, even in the American zone, where we had a free hand to promote our own brand of democracy. Hitler had made things hard for us. He had killed or broken the best of the potential leaders of democracy. Those who had survived were old and found it hard to provide a dynamic leadership adapted to the needs of 1947 rather than those of 1932. All those Germans under about twenty-seven years of age had had a thoroughly Nazi education and had no adult remembrance of the time before Nazism.

There are two sides to denazification: one is the punishment and physical elimination from positions of influence in the administration and economy of the country of men who are actively Nazi or anti-democratic. The other is mental denazification or re-education of the mass of the population. Since education is a slow process, the success of this second part of the programme may not be measurable for a generation.

The first, negative half of the programme has two purposes: to punish the guilty; and to give the country's democratic elements a chance to assert themselves. This involves the removal of their opponents from influential positions. It is a paradox that the Allies are using undemocratic methods to make Germany a democracy. We are in effect trying to force the Germans to be democratic. One responsible military government officer in Berlin is fond of saying: "When the Germans object that our methods are undemocratic, I tell them: 'This is no democracy; this is military government. You will get democracy when you are ready for it!'" The justification for such a procedure is that there may be no alternative. The pre-Hitler democracy allowed its enemies to vote it out of existence; some way must be found to prevent the new German democracy from becoming self-liquidating. The obvious way was to deny the privileges of democracy to those who opposed it.

What is being attempted in the United States zone of Germany is really very simple. We are suspending democracy until we have by admittedly undemocratic methods created the conditions under which we believe democracy can survive and prosper. It is true that the Germans have had free elections (from which parties, candidates and voters considered non-democratic were excluded), and that an increasing measure of self-government has been restored to them. However, the last word always rests with the military government, so what it

51

really amounts to is that the Germans are being given practice in the techniques of democracy.

It is not the American way to forbid any political party or punish people for having adhered to a certain party. Yet in Germany we ban the Nazi party and any other which we arbitrarily decide is undemocratic. Furthermore, we try to punish Germans on the basis of their membership in the Nazi party and its affiliated organizations. The argument is that the Nazi party was not really a political party as we understand the term (Hitler often boasted that it was not), but rather a conspiracy. The conspiracy charge had to be proved. Over 100,000 Germans could not be kept indefinitely in American jails without having charges brought against them. As it was, *habeas corpus* was suspended for over a year while the legal basis for their trial was being established at Nuernberg. Most of those in prison could not be tried for direct participation in atrocities or for any generally recognized crime. They could only be punished as members of a vast conspiracy.

This was one of the main purposes of Nuernberg. It was also designed to impress the guilt of their leaders upon the Germans, and to set the record of Nazism straight for history. Only incidental was the punishment of the actual defendants, most of whom could have been convicted much more rapidly of such recognized crimes as murder, incitement to murder, and theft. In order to prove the complicated case of "conspiracy to commit crimes against peace, war crimes and crimes against humanity" it was necessary to establish new precedents in international law.

The international military tribunal itself was as unprecedented as the crimes upon which it was passing judgment. Many critics disputed the whole legal basis for the trial, their chief points being that the defendants were being tried for crimes which were not crimes at the time they were committed; and that there was no justice in holding a trial of the vanquished by the victors—in other words, that the Nazi leaders were being tried for having lost the war rather than for having started it.

While the charter of the tribunal stated explicitly that the competence of the tribunal was not open to challenge, the chief prosecutors nevertheless went to great pains to justify the legality of this procedure. They put themselves in the peculiar position of trying to prove to the tribunal that it was legal and that it was entitled to judge the crimes it was established to try. The tribunal would hardly have been inclined to require such proofs; but the prosecutors were interested in proving their case for world public opinion and for history.

For instance, Justice Jackson, speaking for the American prosecution, said:

"Unfortunately the nature of these crimes is such that both prosecution and judgment must be by victor nations over vanquished foes. The worldwide scope of the aggressions carried out by these men has left but few real neutrals. Either the victors must judge the vanquished or we must leave the defeated to judge themselves."

Jackson also took pains to prove that aggressive war was a recognized crime:

"The re-establishment of the principle that there are unjust wars and that unjust wars are illegal is traceable in many steps. One of the most significant is the Briand–Kellogg Pact of 1928, by which Germany, Italy and Japan, in common with practically all the nations of the world, renounced war as an instrument of national policy, bound themselves to seek the settlement of disputes by pacific means and condemned recourse to war for the solution of international controversies. This pact altered the legal status of a war of aggression . . .

"A failure of these Nazis to heed, or to understand the force and meaning of this evolution in the legal thought of the world is not a defense or a mitigation. If anything, it aggravates their offense and makes it the more mandatory that the law they have flouted be vindicated by juridical application to their lawless conduct. Indeed by their own law—had they heeded any law—these principles were binding on these defendants. Article 4 of the Weimar Constitution provided that: 'The generally accepted rules of international law are to be considered as binding integral parts of the law of the German Reich.' Can there be any doubt that the outlawry of aggressive war was one of the 'generally accepted rules of international law' in 1939?"

There was a difference between showing that aggressive war was recognized crime and proving that a particular war had been aggressive. Every nation pretends that it acts in self-

53

defence, and if it has made the first overt move it can always argue that this was done to forestall aggression by the other party, that attack is the best defence. In the case of Hitler's war, the prosecution was able to produce telling documents to show that the Nazi aggression had been planned months in advance; but there have been wars and may again be wars in which it is less simple to determine who was the aggressor.

Jackson was particularly concerned about the criticism that there was no legal precedent for trying the Nazi crimes. He said:

"It is true of course that we have no judicial precedent for the Charter (the document creating the Tribunal and defining its functions, duties and prerogatives). But international law is more than a scholarly collection of abstract and immutable principles. It is an outgrowth of treaties and agreements between nations and of accepted customs. Yet every custom has its origin in some single act, and every agreement has to be initiated by the action of some State. Unless we are prepared to abandon every principle of growth for international law, we cannot deny that our own day has the right to institute customs and to conclude agreements that will themselves become sources of a newer and strengthened international law.

"International law is not capable of development by the normal processes of legislation for there is no continuing international legislative authority. Innovations and revisions in international law are brought about by the action of governments designed to meet a change in circumstances. It grows, as did the common law, through decisions reached from time to time in adapting settled principles to new situations. The fact is that when the law evolves by the case method, as did the common law and as international law must do if it is to advance at all, it advances at the expense of those who wrongly guessed the law and learned too late their error. The law, so far as international law can be decreed, had been clearly pronounced when these acts took place. Hence, I am not disturbed by the lack of judicial precedent for the inquiry we propose to conduct."

The American prosecutor was persuasive in his argument against the criticism that the defendants' crimes were not crimes when they were committed and that there was no precedent for creating an international tribunal to try these crimes. It remained to establish conspiracy to commit them, and the concept of criminal conspiracies is nothing new in law. He did not explain satisfactorily why at least one neutral and one German judge might not have been included on the Tribunal. This would surely have done much to convince the world, and particularly the Germans, of the fairness of the trial.

Jackson deserves real commendation for his efforts to get the tribunal established, its procedures agreed upon and the actual trial started. Without these efforts it might never have taken place. The brilliance of his opening statement is likewise worthy of the highest praise. It is to be regretted that he turned the trial into a predominantly American "show"—and in many ways a poor show. A four-Power trial of such immense importance should have been held in Berlin, a four-Power city, instead of in a city of the American zone. The symbolical value of Berlin as the former capital of the Third Reich is as great as that of Nuernberg as the city of the Nazi party congresses.

The American prosecution under Jackson not only put on the show but stole it. The Americans went on first with the most crucial part of the case—the conspiracy charge. They produced all the most sensational documents, including many which would have fitted better into other parts of the case. Having taken over the most important phase of the case, they bungled it. Instead of bringing over the best American legal talent (the British brought theirs), Jackson let the Nuernberg Palace of Justice be used as a kind of proving ground for inexperienced young lawyers. These lawyers did not even achieve their purpose of establishing their reputations at Nuernberg, because the majority of them were bad as well as inexperienced and young.

There was a stunned and embarrassed silence in the palace court room after one of these lawyers, opening his exposition, told the Tribunal: "If you hear a peculiar noise in your earphones, it is not the rustling of documents, but the shaking of my knees. They are trembling as they have not since that other momentous day in my life when I asked the best little woman in the world to be my wife." This startling confession was dutifully rendered into Russian, French and German by the astonished interpreters.

The whole American case was poorly organized. Time and again the American lawyers were interrupted by the extremely able presiding judge, British Lord Justice Lawrence, because

55

their evidence was "redundant and cumulative". Nor did the American staff shine better at cross-examination than at presentation. Jackson came off poorly when he crossed swords with Goering and Schacht.

There is reason to doubt whether the trial succeeded in its propaganda aims. The public, in Germany and abroad, soon became bored with it. The Germans were inclined to admit the guilt of the defendants but to doubt the justice of trying them by Allied judges. One important duplication of the trial was not lost on them, however. If the Nazi leaders were guilty of a conspiracy to seize power, wage war and perpetrate atrocities, then the German people as a whole were absolved of this guilt. Jackson himself had not hesitated to follow his own reasoning through to its logical conclusion. He said:

> "We would also make clear that we have no purpose to incriminate the whole German people. We know that the Nazi party was not put in power by a majority of the German vote. We know it came to power by an evil alliance between the most extreme of the Nazi revolutionists, the most unrestrained of the German reactionaries and the most aggressive of the German militarists. If the German populace had willingly accepted the Nazi programme, no storm troopers would have been needed in the early days of the party and there would have been no need for concentration camps or the Gestapo, both of which institutions were inaugurated as soon as the Nazis gained control of the German state. Only after these lawless innovations proved successful at home were they taken abroad."

The punishment of the imprisoned Nazis in American jails had to wait until the Nuernberg trial had dragged out through the winter and spring and summer. In the meantime the military government could go ahead with the job of removing Nazis from positions of influence. The American denazification policy has been criticized for being too soft and for being too hard.

There has been some justification for both charges. In the early months in Bavaria, Nazis and men with Nazi ideas were left in high administrative posts. Friedrich Schaeffer, the American-appointed minister president, was the chief of the right wing of the conservative Christian Social Union (successor to the Catholic Bavarian People's party). In pre-Hitler days he and his party had, to use an understatement, done little to combat the Nazis. Five months after the occupation of Munich it was discovered that twenty active Nazis still held high posts in Schaeffer's administration. General Patton knew about this situation, tolerated it and refrained from carrying out General Eisenhower's denazification directives.

It was Patton's statement about "this Nazi thing" that brought about his dismissal and that of Schaeffer (who had previously offered to resign but had been requested by Third Army Military Government not to do so).

The Patton–Schaeffer scandal precipitated the issue of a new denazification law—the famous Law No. 8. Previous directives had not gone beyond the internment of Nazis in "mandatory arrest" categories and the purge of the civil administration and police. The new law extended to the field of business and industry. Such a law had already been under consideration; it was hurriedly drafted and published in order to appease public opinion in the States, indignant at the reports from Bavaria.

Law No. 8 provided that "it shall be unlawful for any business enterprise to employ any member of the Nazi party or of its affiliate organizations in any supervisory or managerial capacity, or otherwise than in ordinary labor". It was received with consternation by the Germans, who saw in it a plan for ruining their economy. It was, of course, not intended in this way; but it had been drawn up so hurriedly that it might well have had this effect if it had been literally applied. Two weeks were taken to interpret it so that discretion could be used in the case of "nominal" Nazis. German appeal courts were set up, subject to control by the military government.

The real dilemma facing the Allied authorities was the thoroughness with which the Nazis had taken over the important positions in government and industry. It would have been impossible to find replacements for all Nazis in such positions. It was necessary, therefore, to determine which ones had joined the party under pressure—for instance, in order to keep their jobs.

The United States was the only country that operated on the principle that efficiency in administration and higher production were not valid reasons for keeping Nazis in positions of influence, even as a temporary measure. The British made the greatest compromise in this respect. I can give two extreme examples that came to my attention.

More than a year after the occupation, Dr. Richard Sallett, a former official of the Press Department of the Foreign Office, known to all American correspondents who worked in Berlin at the beginning of the war as a particularly offensive type of Nazi, was in a position in the British zone where he had the authority to pass on applicants for admission to institutes of higher learning. And Werner Asendorb, a former Propaganda Ministry official, was kept by the British in a responsible editorial position on their newspaper in Berlin, even after they had been shown proof that he had been an active Nazi.

The French also were happy to employ Germans who had been dismissed by the Americans under their denazification policy. The Russians were content to eliminate the top Nazis and control the others. Their zone was the first one in which the "kleine P.G.'s", or small Nazis, were given full rights and permitted to join political parties. The Russians did not want to create a large disgruntled group, forced into opposition by discrimination and exclusion from the life of the community. They were also anxious to win the small Nazis for the Soviet-sponsored Socialist Unity party, and they sometimes made use of Nazis who were not so "small".

Stories about the inconsistencies of denazification flew all over Germany. One example will be sufficient here. In Wiesbaden a fairly well-dressed man was cleaning a street with an ineptitude that made it apparent that he was unused to this type of activity. A bystander kept offering him suggestions on how to improve his technique, and finally commented: "It's obvious that you're no street-cleaner; how do you happen to be in this job, anyway?"

"I was the director of a large hospital," was the answer, "but I lost my job because I was a Nazi." He then asked the bystander: "What do you do? You seem to know quite a lot about this job."

"Of course. I used to be a street-cleaner, but I lost my job because I was a Nazi."

The story, if not true, is certainly possible. A correspondent in Berlin was actually told by the military government to dismiss his charwoman because she had been in the Nazi party. Apparently it is considered a special privilege to do even the lowest form of menial labour for the Americans.

The chief fault of the American approach to denazification was the attempt to put everyone into categories. It sounds easy to say "get rid of the Nazis", but there were all degrees of Nazis. There were those who joined under pressure, there were the opportunists, there were the "idealistic" Nazis who later became disillusioned and fell away, there were people who had supported the Nazis and profited under the Nazi regime but had never signed a membership card. The Americans lacked the personnel to inquire into the individual merits of each case; hence the category system under which the Germans were required to fill out lengthy "Fragebogen" or questionnaires and were classified on the basis of their answers.

The Special Branches had processed over 1,000,000 such questionnaires by the end of 1945. Of the cases considered, 18 per cent were in the worst category—non-employment mandatory; 7 per cent fell into Category II—employment discretionary, adverse recommendation; and 24 per cent in Category III—employment discretionary, no adverse recommendation. The largest group was Category IV—no evidence of Nazi activity (50 per cent); and the smallest was Category V—evidence of anti-Nazi activity (only 1 per cent).

The magnitude of the job and the shortage of qualified American personnel were bound sooner or later to force the American authorities to turn denazification over to the Germans. This happened in March, 1946, when a uniform "Law for the Liberation from National Socialism and Militarism" was submitted by the minister presidents of the three Laender or States of the American zone and approved by General Clay. The objectives of the law were described as:

(1) to provide just and effective procedures for judging every individual according to the degree of his responsibility for the wrongs committed by the Nazi regime;

(2) to impose upon those found responsible definite sanctions designed to eliminate their influence in the community;

(3) to provide opportunities for rehabilitation through probation for lesser offenders; and

(4) to remove disqualifications from followers (nominal Nazis) and exonerated persons.

General Clay estimated that between 1,500,000 and 2,000,000 persons in the American zone out of a population of

16,000,000 would be affected. Their cases would be reviewed, and might be brought before one of 400 tribunals to be established throughout the zone. Every citizen would be required to register, and must produce evidence that he had done so in order to be able to draw his food rations.

It is interesting to note that terms in labour camps could be imposed and single or recurring fines set, on the basis of rank or membership in various Nazi organizations. This was done before these organizations had been declared criminal by the Nuernberg tribunal. Some of them never were so declared. The legal basis for the procedure was that criminal sentences were not being imposed, but that the Nazis were being required to make a special contribution to reparations in the form of money or labour. This would not preclude their being prosecuted as war criminals. Lesser offenders would pay a small fine and could then resume their place in the community without fear of further discrimination.

It was obvious that the Americans would have been unable to complete such a comprehensive denazification programme; it was somewhat dubious whether the Germans could. An enormous amount of time would be taken up in the consideration of each individual case by the tribunals. At the end of five months only 38,062 charges had been filed and only 8,367 cases had been terminated. The Bavarian Minister for Political Liberation had to be dismissed. Finally, eight months after the law was passed, Clay had to rebuke the three minister presidents publicly for their failure to denazify quickly and effectively. The theory of trying the Nazis by their neighbours was a good one if the right people could be found. If the men on the tribunals were not influenced by personal rancour and were themselves clear of any Nazi taint, they would be in a better position than any American to judge of the merits of individual cases. Unfortunately it was not easy to get the best men for these jobs. They knew that after a year or two they would have to look around for another job, and their popularity was not likely to have grown.

There was one more problem: while the Allied Control Council had passed a denazification law, in an attempt to secure uniform policies, none of the other Powers had gone as far as the Americans in implementing the law. If Germany were eventually unified, it might prove impossible to keep several hundred thousand Nazis in prisons and labour camps in

60

the American zone when this was not being done in other zones. In an important matter like denazification, uniform practices as well as uniform policies are essential. It is equally essential to make sure that the chief offenders do not escape their just punishment either because of technical difficulties or because of lack of agreement among the occupying Powers.

IV
FOOD AND DEMOCRACY

NEWS PICTURE

. . . GERMANS TOLD OF FAMINE PERIL BY EISENHOWER . . . *broadcast instructions today to farmers in western germany to stay on the land refuse to be conscripted into the volksturm* . . . 3-WAY BERLIN RULE AWAITS FOOD ACCORD . . . US AND BRITAIN SEND FIRST FOOD TRAIN TO BERLIN . . . BERLINS RATION CARDS EXCEED FOOD SUPPLIES . . .

. . . recalled the nazi atrocities in concentration camps and american casualties resulting from prolonged german resistance in the war and said if any place is to blame for the destructions and calamities of this war it is berlin we are bringing food here not because we like to feed the germans but because we don't want their rotten corpses to infect our troops . . .

. . . BERLINERS SEE INFLATION THREAT IN ALLIED MARKS . . . 12 MILLION GERMANS MIGRATE WEST . . . 850,000 GERMANS IN US ZONE WILL BE VACCINATED . . . PATTON AND ZHUKOV TAKE SALUTES OF 5 MILE VJ PARADE IN BERLIN . . .

. . . patton made his appearance five minutes ahead of zhukov driving up with an escort of four motorcycles two military police jeeps and five sedans he was conspicuous in his burnished helmetliner pink ridingbreeches highly-polished boots pistol white gloves and swaggerstick the redarmy marshal who commands all soviet forces in germany arrived with less circumstance his open black packard was unescorted but his uniform rivaled pattons his was a bluegreen with visored cap of the same color rimmed with scarlet and decorated with gold braid the most striking feature of his formal attire was the panoply of glittering medals that covered and literally hid both sides of his chest right down to his white belt . . .

. . . The normal consumer has been on a 1,000 calorie starvation diet for nearly three months the germans have been getting some food in addition to the ration the officer said people cannot live on 1,000 calories he asserted thats a fact if the germans had been living on 1,000 calories since the ration cut speaking broadly they would all be dead . . .

In Berlin children gathered the acorns as they fell from the oaks that lined the sidewalks. Later they swept up the dead leaves and took them home to burn. Old women and young boys carefully filled pails with the horse-manure from the street; picked cigarette butts out of the gutter and took them home to dry them and extract the tobacco; got up early to take their carts into the park and pile them with dead branches and twigs; and crowded on to the suburban lines to ride out beyond Potsdam to barter with the peasants for potatoes with which they filled their knapsacks. After school the small girls lined up outside the enlisted men's mess. Sometimes they watched the mess sergeant pour the left-over cocoa down the drain (Army regulations forbid giving American food to Germans). But if the sergeant were kind-hearted and nobody was looking he might fill their containers with the slop of uneaten pieces of bread, bits of fat, canned vegetables, mixed in with soup and coffee—all the waste that had been whisked from the men's plates into the large garbage can.

.   .   .   .   .

Ingeborg was not a promiscuous girl. When she was eighteen, Hans had been called up to be sent to the Eastern Front. Before he left she had, with some trepidation but without too much reluctance, given him what he seemed to want so badly. She didn't think there was anything wrong about it: most girls in Germany seemed to do it, and then there was a kind of understanding that they would get married "after the war". She hoped it had made him happy because to her it had been rather disappointing—painful and sordid rather than romantic. She liked it better when he came back on furlough a year later.

After a while she stopped hearing from him and he never came back again. Instead the Russians came: she hid in the cellar for four days, and when she came out she began to hear awful stories about what had happened to some of her girl friends. Two months later the Americans came. By this time she had lost eight pounds, which really improved her appearance—but she was tired of going to bed hungry at night.

Joe was a tall corporal who wore his soiled cap high on his head and walked in a careless, self-confident, lurching way and had an interesting-looking triangular coloured patch with a tank and a number two on his sleeve and four new medal ribbons on his chest. The first evening he called her Babe and gave her cigarettes and said she was the cutest thing he had seen in Germany and he could really go for her. She didn't quite understand all this American talk, but she got the general idea when he said, "Listen, Babe. How about you and me going steady? I dunno how long I'll be stationed here, but I won't look at another babe, honest I won't, and all you gotta do is play square with me and I got beaucoup cigarettes and chocolate; I got an in with the mess sergeant, and I'll take care of you good, honest I will, 'cause I can really go for you in a big way."

She was a little scared, and said she didn't know, and anyway not to-night. He went back and told his buddy, "Say, I gotta swell shack job lined up. She wouldn't come through to-night, but they generally don't the first night; it's in the bag for to-morrow." It was. At first she had to sneak him into the house, but pretty soon her mother found out and there was a row, but it was finally straightened out and her mother was reconciled to the idea, and said Joe seemed like a nice boy; but what she meant was that she liked the K-rations he brought, and her father was glad to be able to pick up the cigarette butts in Ingeborg's room in the morning.

One day two months later Joe said, "Listen, honey. We're gettin' moved outa here in a coupla days. Gee, I'm sorry I gotta leave you, 'cause you been swell, but that's the Army." She cried, and he promised to write, and gave her a whole case of K-rations and a carton of cigarettes.

After that she was unhappy for a week, but then she met Ted, who was a lieutenant and wore parachute wings and had a different kind of patch on his sleeve. When she started to tell him about how her girl friends had been raped by the Russians he told her to shut up, the Russkis were O.K. and he'd heard enough of that line (but one evening about a month later he came along very mad and told her how the damn Russkis had shot one of the men in his outfit, who was up in the 279th right now, and they didn't know whether he would pull through).

She didn't dare take Ted home right away because she knew her parents wouldn't think it was right so soon after Joe. But Ted said he had a swell lay-out, and took her up to his room. She was embarrassed at first because he was sharing it with another officer who had another girl, but Ted said, "Hell! don't worry about Jim; he's not going to pay any attention to us, he's got his own business to attend to." After a few nights all four of them got very friendly and the whole thing seemed perfectly natural. She liked it better than with Joe because Ted took her to dances and had whole meals brought up to his room, which was better than K-rations, which she was getting pretty tired of anyway.

When Ted left there was Frank, and then Steve, and then Red. Ted was the only one she really enjoyed sleeping with: the others were perfunctory about it, and were usually drunk as well. She confided once to a girl friend that she didn't think Americans were very good lovers, and her girl friend said No, but it was better than being hungry, wasn't it?

.   .   .   .   .

The fact that Germans are hungry is something that one lives with if one lives in Germany. It creates an atmosphere of depression and futility from which even the well-fed occupying forces cannot escape. And it has profoundly influenced occupation policies and relations among the Allies.

Food is politics in Germany. When the Russians brought vegetables into Berlin from the surrounding countryside, that was politics. The news got banner headlines in the Russian-controlled section of the Press, and the fact that the food went to the Western sectors as well as the Soviet sector of Berlin was not omitted. When rations were slashed in the British and American zones, or when hundreds of thousands of tons of wheat were shipped into western Germany from the United States and Canada, political repercussions were inevitable.

Food is politics in Germany because it is a propaganda trump. It is politics in another sense as well, in the sense that the programme of teaching the Germans democracy must fail unless the Germans are adequately fed. As the British General Robertson said:

"A famished Germany will be a prey to the influences which are ever ready to pounce upon the miserable and discontented. . . . *One cannot hope to reform the heart of the German people unless one keeps their stomach reasonably full.*"

What "influences" General Robertson had in mind I cannot say. He may well have been thinking of the Communists as much as of a possible revival of Nazism under some other name. I do know that many British and American leaders believed one reason the Russians would not agree to pool food resources (their zone being relatively well off in this respect) was that they hoped Communism would benefit from starvation in western Germany.

To many Americans, bringing food into western Germany meant protecting it against Communism as well as against a revival of Nazism. Others did not think we should help feed the Germans as long as surrounding countries did not have enough to eat. We really had no choice, however. By coming into Germany and taking over the functions of government, we had assumed responsibility for the German people. We had to prevent starvation. Incidentally, that was all we were able to do. . . . Few European countries had less to eat than Germany.

The Germans have been depicted to Americans by some observers as starving, by others as being so well fed that there was no need to worry about them. It is pertinent to ask exactly how badly off they are.

I would answer that by saying that in the first eighteen months of the occupation most Germans were hungry; but few starved. Leaving the farmers out of account, the average German has almost forgotten what it is like to have a full stomach, not to worry about the next meal. He is constantly preoccupied with the question of food: it is his primary concern.

The starvation that exists is mainly indirect starvation, except in the Ruhr, where there has been real famine. Nutritional diseases and tuberculosis are rising at an alarming rate. Infant mortality is higher, the old and the sick die more quickly. People do not keel over and die in the streets of starvation (as Athenians did under the German occupation), but they fall easy prey to disease because their resistance is lower. In Berlin in the first six months of 1946 the death rate was six times the birth rate, the difference between the two rates being such as to reduce the city's population from 3,000,000 to 2,000,000 in fifteen years, if maintained.

Visitors on flying trips to Germany have sometimes, after taking a look at the Germans in the streets, pronounced their opinion that they looked well fed and that all the talk of hunger must be misplaced sympathy. General Robertson emphasized the necessity for scepticism in evaluating such reports when he told a Press conference:

"Certain casual observers have, after a short survey, given publicity to their impression that the Germans are doing nicely. Of course the farm population is relatively well fed. No one has ever devised a system whereby farmers could be made to conform strictly to a universal low ration. The children, too, are reasonably healthy because we have taken special measures to safeguard them. But the reports of nutrition experts are the only reliable reports and they have never confirmed the rosy accounts given by some of our guests.

"The latest report that comes from the Anglo–American–French Committee which has just made a survey of urban areas in the American, French and British Zones in February (1946) shows that there has not been any serious deterioration in the health of most normal consumers. Nevertheless in this report the Committee said: 'It is imperative that the recommended ration scales be achieved and maintained until the next harvest season. Experience has already shown that ration levels less than those recommended by this Committee produce malnutrition which may reach alarming proportions in a relatively short period of time.' "

This statement was made at the time of the British announcement that they had cut the ration in their zone from 1,500 to 1,000 calories.

It is often misleading to state food consumption in terms of calories. The breakdown into proteins, fats and starches is also important, as is the quantity of vitamins in the diet. Moreover, it is impossible to know how much a consumer is getting in addition to his official ration. Calories are merely useful as a rough guide. In the United States the average consumption is estimated at from 3,200 to 3,500 calories. In July, 1946, the normal consumer (non-worker) in the American zone was entitled to food equivalent to 1,185 calories.

Thus a housewife with one child could draw every day 5 oz. of bread (say, five medium slices), just under 1 lb. of potatoes, $\frac{3}{4}$ oz. of other starches, $\frac{5}{8}$ oz. of fat, $\frac{5}{16}$ oz. of sugar, $1\frac{1}{4}$ oz. of meat, $\frac{5}{16}$ oz. of cheese, $1\frac{1}{4}$ cups of skim milk, $\frac{1}{4}$ oz. of milk powder, $\frac{1}{4}$ oz. of egg powder, $\frac{1}{8}$ oz. of dried onions, $1\frac{1}{4}$ oz. of fresh fish and $\frac{1}{8}$ oz. of "ersatz" coffee.

If she were pregnant, this housewife would get an allotment of whole milk, and if her child were under six years old, he, too, would get whole milk (but less of other items). If her husband were a heavy worker he would draw a considerably higher ration. Since the family's food would be pooled, the mother and child would actually be eating some of the father's ration. They would be less hungry but he would work less well. The family might also have a vegetable garden. It might get food packages from relatives in the country, or the mother might go out and trade some of her clothes or household possessions to farmers for food. The farmers were supposed to sell their produce at official prices for distribution to the urban population. Since the prices were low, and there was little to buy on the open market, there was not a strong inducement for them to do this, and enforcement was naturally difficult.

I saw the people of Berlin in 1940 and again in 1945. There is no doubt that they had lost weight. Many of them looked better for it; by 1945 it was a rarity to see a fat person, whereas formerly too many Germans had been unattractively obese. In 1940 I had a cook who had grown corpulent from eating her own dishes. I ran into her on the street one day five years later and did not recognize her. She had lost 81 lb. It had improved her figure, although no doubt the process had been painful. Other Germans, with less of a reserve to fall back on, suffered more. The old people in particular looked pitifully emaciated.

With every German using all his ingenuity to tap every available source for supplementing his ration, it was impossible to tell how much the average consumer was actually eating. One could only generalize and say that they were keeping up to the subsistence level but were not eating enough for full working efficiency. Even the subsistence level was maintained, in western Germany, only by considerable imports of food. The Germans had no immediate way of paying for these imports and few prospects of being able to do so in the foreseeable future. The imports were entered on the books, but in effect western Germany was on the dole.

This state of affairs was the result of necessity: it had not originally been our policy to feed the Germans. A month before V-E Day, General Eisenhower told the Germans in a broadcast from SHAEF: "This year Germany must depend on her own food resources." It was against American policy to use American food to feed Germans.

Three months later it became apparent that this policy would have to be changed. Germany had always been a food-importing country. Within Germany, the western part of the country was a deficit area. For instance, the British zone, even in normal times, produced only about 50 per cent of its food

68

requirements. In the spring of 1945 western Germany had been a battlefield, and the harvest that year was poorer than in any of the previous war years.

By the autumn of that year the British were importing 40 per cent of the food distributed as rations in their zone. They had to pay for this food in dollars, and it was not easy for them to do this. The Americans, in the ten months beginning August 1, 1945, distributed over 600,000 short tons of food in Germany—61 per cent from Army stocks and 39 per cent from direct imports. For Berlin alone the American contribution to the Allied food pool during this period amounted to $50,000,000.

Why did the Allies go to all this expense and trouble to feed the people who had until so recently been their enemies and who for five years had let the populations of most of the other European countries go hungry? The answer was given, again, by General Robertson. He said:

"The problem of food for Germany should be viewed from a practical and not from a sentimental point of view. The Germans have brought this situation on themselves and indeed on the world. We consider that they should be adequately fed, not because we are sorry for them, but as a matter of policy.

"It is no part of British policy to starve Germany, nor is it Allied policy. To do so would be to defeat one of the principal objectives of our occupation, namely, that the German people should be given the opportunity to prepare for the eventual reconstruction of their life on a democratic basis."

Robertson did not say, though he may have had it in mind, that food was closely linked to international politics. This became inevitable from the moment that the Allies failed to establish a common ration in Germany. Such a proposal, made by the Americans in the summer of 1945, was considered untimely by the other three Powers. Russian propaganda made capital of the ration cuts in the western zones, pointing to the land reform (redistribution of the large estates) in their own zone. The Americans and British publicized the contributions they were making by bringing food into Germany, contrasting it with the Russian (and French) policy of requisitioning German food for their troops.

The Russian practice of milking the German economy

largely nullified the effects of their food propaganda. The Germans knew how much they were getting to eat, and no propaganda, however clever, could make them believe they were eating more than they were. The Russians felt justified in sending a large proportion of the German livestock population to Russia to replace what the Germans had taken from them during the war. They felt their occupation army was entitled to eat German food in Germany. They felt their troops had a right to drink vodka made from German potatoes. Russia's Allies might not have disputed these Russian reparations claims; they did object to the Russian manner of doing it without accounting for what they took and without setting any limits to what they proposed to take.

Apart from this, the Russians were removing the bases of their own food propaganda. They had a great opportunity in that their zone was the only one in Germany which could be approximately self-supporting. The Germans in the Soviet zone could have been the best fed, and this would have been a big talking point.

Actually the food situation in the Russian zone was very spotty. In Thuringia and Saxony the Germans undoubtedly ate as well as in most parts of western Germany and better than in distressed areas like the Ruhr. But there were also "hunger belts" in the Russian zone, notably along the Polish border and in the immediate vicinity of Berlin, where the Germans were often unable to draw the food to which their ration cards entitled them. The grim reports that came into Berlin from the surrounding country help to explain the exaggerated stories that went to the States about famine in the Russian zone. Many reporters assumed that the situation in Brandenburg was typical of the whole zone; others were only too glad to send any kind of anti-Soviet story.

Meanwhile western Germany was having its own troubles. The principle of shipping food to Germany to prevent starvation was quickly accepted by the Americans and British. It was soon evident, however, that there would not be enough food to be shipped. By the beginning of 1946 it had become obvious that there was a world shortage of wheat, and that the end of the war had not brought automatic relief. On the contrary, the world food situation appeared more serious than at any time during the war.

The Combined Food Board sat in Washington and toyed

with figures. Droughts had resulted in harvests far below expectations in the great wheat-producing countries. Requirements from deficit areas were larger than anticipated. Everywhere there was a shortage of fertilizers. The war had caused not only devastation but complete disruption of the global agricultural economy. For the critical pre-harvest period between March and July, 1946, the Combined Food Board had received requirements of 20,000,000 tons of wheat and it had only 12,000,000 tons available.

The United States tossed away a great opportunity to show real leadership. By tightening their belts, Americans could have relieved hunger in Allied and former enemy nations alike. With famine threatening large areas of the world, the United States blithely went about ending food rationing and headed for a return to normalcy. Hundreds of thousands of tons of wheat were lost to U.N.R.R.A. because the Congress had not passed the necessary appropriation when the wheat was on the market, and the Department of Agriculture would not take the responsibility of buying up the wheat and holding it. By the time the money was appropriated, the wheat was no longer to be bought.

Europeans knew that Americans were eating well. Wherever there were American troops, there was the unconcealable contrast between the well-fed and the hungry. This was not confined to Germany and Austria, though in those countries the contrast was sharper, more glaring. In France and England and Belgium, too, Americans were the "haves" and the local population were the "have nots". The fact that the average American soldier was generous with his surplus rations did not lessen the general resentment against a nation whose people could live in plenty when most of the rest of the world was needy. It was not only in Germany that American contributions were regarded as an incomplete fulfilment of a moral obligation rather than a big-hearted gift calling for gratitude.

When the crisis came, it was natural that the Allied nations which needed food should come before Germany. It was just as natural that the American authorities who were responsible for military government in Germany should make every effort to put their hands on the food they needed to maintain what they considered was a minimum ration there.

With this in mind, Clay flew to Washington in November, 1945, and secured a promise of enough wheat to maintain a ration of 1,550 calories for the normal consumer until the summer harvest. He came back to Germany and suggested to the minister presidents of the three States in the American zone that they raise the ration to that level. They were reluctant to do so because they feared the effects on public morale if it were subsequently necessary to reduce the ration again. They were in favour of husbanding their stocks and increasing the ration later on if conditions warranted. Clay was anxious to give the people more food during the winter, and said he could commit the American Government to maintaining the higher ration.

Within two months the deterioration in the world food situation had become so obvious that all estimates had to be revised. Clay found out he would not get the wheat he had been promised, and for a long time he was not told how much he would get. A flow of about 100,000 tons of wheat a month during the first six months of 1946 would have been required to support the 1,550-calorie ration. There was none forthcoming during the first three months of that period, and only 50,000 tons a month during the second three months. The ration had to be reduced twice, to a low of 1,180 calories. The failure of the United States to live up to its commitment was a bad blow to American prestige.

Of more basic significance was the failure of the four Allies to agree on common food policies for Germany. The pooling of all food resources in the country and their distribution by a central German food administration would not have created more food, but it would certainly have meant a more efficient and more equitable distribution. Moreover, a situation should not have been permitted to develop where food became a political weapon, used by the Allies to compete with one another for the favour of the Germans.

Food was the most pressing of the economic problems in Germany, but it was only one of many. Eighteen months after the complete collapse of the German economy, it had made but a very slow start towards recovery. It was, in fact, misleading to talk of a German economy at all: the divisions between the Allies had caused a division of Germany into zones whose frontiers were economic barriers as well as demarcation lines for the occupation troops.

J.C.S. 1067, the basic directive on military government policy sent to General Eisenhower by the Joint Chiefs of Staff before the capitulation of Germany, stated: "You will take no steps (*a*) looking toward the economic rehabilitation of Germany or (*b*) designed to maintain or strengthen the German economy". Exceptions to this principle were authorized only "to protect the safety and meet the needs of the occupying forces and assure the production and maintenance of goods and services required to prevent starvation or such disease and unrest as would endanger these forces".

At the time this directive was written it was apparently feared that the war would leave the German economy healthy enough so that it would be dangerous to strengthen, or even to maintain it. Any such fears were unfounded. The German economy after six years of war effort had broken down completely. While the main purpose of the occupation was to prevent it from reviving sufficiently to support another war, the immediate concern of the occupiers had to be to restore a semblance of normal conditions and put life on some kind of a running basis. In the American zone this could be done by using a broad interpretation of the clause about protecting the safety of the occupying forces and preventing starvation, disease and unrest. Nobody could predict to what extent it would be necessary to rehabilitate the German economy in order to prevent disease and unrest. It was up to the Military Governor to use his own judgment.

When the economic life of a highly industrialized country comes almost to a standstill, it is not easy to get it going again. Transport and communications are disrupted. The value of the currency is dubious. Sources of raw materials are shut off. There are few consumer goods on the market.

In Germany there was a whole series of vicious circles. For instance, the farmers would have had more incentive to produce more food and sell it at legal prices if there had been more goods on the market for them to buy. There would have been more goods produced if the workers had not been short of food. This was particularly true of coal-mining. A man doing strenuous work of this type tires quickly if he is not getting enough food. When the ration was reduced in the British zone, there was an immediate and sharp drop in the Ruhr coal production. While the miners did get special rations, there was no effective way of preventing them from sharing their food with their families. Less coal from the Ruhr meant less coal for the liberated countries of Europe, which relied on German coal exports. It also meant less coal for other German industries.

The allocation of coal to the German economy was already so small that it was insufficient to support even the industries manufacturing needed products for the mines. The crippling of the consumer-goods industries, largely as a result of the coal shortage, in turn reacted on coal production because the miners' morale was lowered and their incentive taken away by the lack of goods on the market.

Another vicious circle revolved around the currency. As long as Germans lacked confidence in the mark and feared it

Industry.	Unit.	Pre-war average.	July, 1946.	Permitted Production under Allied Plan.
Fertilizers.				
Cyanimid	Tons N_2	4,400	3,425	3,750
Other Nitrogen Compounds	Tons N_2	2,200	1,300	—
Phosphates	Tons P_2O_5	1,650	294	2,000
Thomas Slag	Tons P_2O_5	550	510	—
Potash	Tons K_2O	14,600	16,310	20,000
Soda Ash	Tons	3,200	4,710	14,000
Sulphuric Acid	Tons SO_3	—	2,200	12,500
Soap	Tons	—	941	2,200
Building Materials.				
Cement	Tons ('000)	235	103	183
Glass	Sq. M. ('000)	575	515	No limit
Lime	Tons ('000)	762	28	,,
Lumber	Cu. M. ('000)	317	255	,,
Plaster	Tons	28,500	5,431	,,
Roofing Tile	('000)	30,167	13,622	,,
Roofing Paper	Sq. M. ('000)	5,042	838	,,
Bricks	('000)	229,167	28,528	,,
Anti-Friction Bearings	Tons	2,218	469	—
Construction Machinery	Tons	1,268	364	—
Trucks		1,686	142	1,420
Automobiles		14,842	0	1,670
Motor-cycles		10,000	131	670
Light Bulbs	('000)	500	304	2,000
Radio Receivers		12,000	1,663	2,750
Electric Motors	H.P.	130,000	26,900	100,000
Storage Batteries		20,000	5,897	9,000
Dry Batteries		80,000	60,864	200,000
Tractors		2,070	105	No limit
Threshers		2,270	123	,,
Harrows		13,813	538	,,
Ploughs		34,271	1,301	,,
Cameras (except Box Cameras)		65,000	11,107	65,000
Binoculars		—	4,765	7,500
Yarn	Tons	10,730	2,656	5,891
Synthetic Fibres	Tons	1,479	1,154	4,641
Cloth (Finishing Output)	Tons	9,054	2,896	5,650
Household and Decorative Porcelain	Tons	4,400	800	No limit
Shoes	('000 pairs)	3,708	972	3,000
Stoves	('000)	63	46	Not established

would lose its value, they were reluctant to sell their goods or produce new ones; and the lack of goods further depressed the real value of their money.

In the American zone the coal shortage was the main factor in limiting production. Ours was the only one of the four zones without any appreciable coal resources. Under a quadripartite arrangement, it got an allocation of coal from the other zones. This was just sufficient for the needs of the Army, public utilities, hospitals and the most essential industries.

By July, 1946, production in even these essential industries was still well below the modest level permitted by the Allied level of industry plan, as the table on p. 74 shows. (This plan, which set ceilings on German production in key industries, will be considered in detail in the next chapter.)

The second important factor limiting production, after the extraction of coal, was the difficulty of obtaining raw materials. Germany was a highly integrated country, and the artificially-drawn zonal boundaries often put the materials needed for a certain product in two or more zones. Or the raw materials might be in one zone, the coal in another, the processing plants in a third and the assembly plants in a fourth. Some factories were able to resume production by using stocks on hand, but by the end of the first year these were dwindling, if not exhausted. Every month the restrictive effect of the division of Germany into zones that could never be economically self-sufficient became more noticeable.

Increasingly the Germans, who at first showed some readiness to admit that their economic plight could be blamed on the Nazi regime and its war, felt inclined to shift that blame on to the inability of the Allies to agree on policies for running Germany. And it was true that while the Germans had nobody but themselves and their former Government to blame for their plight at the end of the war, the prolongation and even deterioration of Germany's desperate situation were traceable to Allied disunity.

HARD PEACE OR SOFT?

News Picture

TOP SECRET
J.C.S. 1067/6
26 *April* 1945

JOINT CHIEFS OF STAFF
DIRECTIVE TO COMMANDER IN CHIEF OF U.S. FORCES OF OCCUPATION REGARDING THE MILITARY GOVERNMENT OF GERMANY

4. Basic Objectives of Military Government in Germany :

a. It should be brought home to the Germans that Germany's ruthless warfare and fanatical Nazi resistance have destroyed the German economy and made chaos and suffering inevitable and that the Germans cannot escape responsibility for what they have brought upon themselves.

b. Germany will not be occupied for the purpose of liberation but as a defeated enemy nation. Your aim is not oppression but to occupy Germany for the purpose of realizing certain important Allied objectives. In the conduct of your occupation and administration you should be just but·firm and aloof. You will strongly discourage fraternization with the German officials and population.

c. The principal Allied objective is to prevent Germany from ever again becoming a threat to the peace of the world. Essential steps in the accomplishment of this objective are the elimination of Nazism and militarism in all their forms, the immediate apprehension of war criminals for punishment, the industrial disarmament and demilitarization of Germany, with continuing control over Germany's capacity to make war, and the preparation for an eventual reconstruction of German political life on a democratic basis.

d. Other Allied objectives are to enforce the program of reparations and restitution, to provide relief for the benefit of countries devastated by Nazi aggression, and to ensure that prisoners of war and displaced persons of the United Nations are cared for and repatriated.

8. Suspected War Criminals and Security Arrests :

a. You will search out, arrest, and hold, pending receipt by you of further instructions as to their disposition, Adolf Hitler, his chief Nazi

76

associates, other war criminals and all persons who have participated in planning or carrying out Nazi enterprises involving or resulting in atrocities or war crimes.

   b. *All persons who, if permitted to remain at large, would endanger the accomplishment of your objectives will also be arrested and held in custody until trial by an appropriate semi-judicial body to be established by you . . .*

9. *Political Activities :*

   a. *No political activities of any kind shall be countenanced unless authorized by you. You will assure that your military government does not become committed to any political group.*

21. *German Standard of Living :*

   You will estimate requirements of supplies necessary to prevent starvation or widespread disease or such civil unrest as would endanger the occupying forces. . . . You will take no action that would tend to support basic living standards in Germany on a higher level than that existing in any one of the neighbouring United Nations and you will take appropriate measures to ensure that basic living standards of the German people are not higher than those existing in any one of the neighboring United Nations when such measures will contribute to raising the standards of any such nation.

22. *You will urge upon the Control Council that uniform ration scales be applied throughout Germany, that essential items be distributed equitably among the zones, that net surpluses be made available for export to Allied countries, and that imports be limited to the net deficits of Germany as a whole.*

   IT IS ANTICIPATED THAT SUBSTANTIALLY SIMILAR DIRECTIVES WILL BE ISSUED TO THE COMMANDERS IN CHIEF OF THE U.K., U.S.S.R. AND FRENCH FORCES OF OCCUPATION.

I T was a bleak, raw day, New Year's Eve, 1945. Tall, helmeted American sentries, in uniforms that were trim and soldierly enough to satisfy General McNarney that his colleagues on the Allied Control Council would be properly impressed, mounted guard before the sombre Prussian law court that had been converted into the headquarters of four-Power Government in Germany. Inside, in the large main conference room, a score of men sat around a hollow square of tables. One delegation on each side of the square, mostly generals in uniforms liberally decked with rows of medal ribbons (all but the Russians, who wore none), a few diplomats in business suits.

Only four of the men could speak: for the United States, General Clay; for the Soviet Union, General Sokolovsky; for France, General Koeltz; and for Britain, General Templer (deputizing for the absent General Robertson). All the other delegation members could do was give whispered advice to their chiefs or pass over notes with suggestions. After every spoken sentence came a pause while it was translated into the two other languages by interpreters standing behind the speaker.

The Allied Co-ordinating Committee in this meeting was trying to do nothing less ambitious than plan the future economy of Germany. The four generals were discussing steel. They knew the importance to the German war effort of a steel production which in 1943 reached a peak of 27,000,000 tons. They knew that they must reduce German steel capacity to a level which could not conceivably, at any time in the foreseeable future, support such a war effort again.

They knew also that the lower the figure they set, the higher would be the amount of steel plant to be taken from Germany as reparations. At least two of the countries represented at the meeting had a direct interest in these reparations.

The men knew also that there was some limit below which they could not cut German steel capacity (in the prosperity year, 1929, Germany had produced over 18,000,000 tons of steel; in the depression year, 1932, the figure had shrunk to 7,200,000). They had been charged not only with eliminating production that might constitute war potential and with providing reparations, but also with balancing the German economy at a level that would provide the Germans with a reasonable standard of living. These objectives had somehow to be reconciled. So had the views of the several delegations, each of which had a different opinion about what constituted a war potential and what was necessary to a peace-time economy.

The Russian member, General Sokolovsky—a youthful, black-haired staff officer—started the ball rolling. He suggested that the Committee take the League of Nations figure for per capita steel consumption in Europe in 1938. This figure—75·2 kilograms—multiplied by the population of Germany, which he estimated at 62,000,000, would give a figure of 4,600,000. He maintained that any amount over that figure would represent war potential and should be removed for reparations.

Each of the other delegates then stated his position. The British General Templer, whose original estimate had been 10,500,000, came down to 9,000,000 and finally, after considerable bargaining, to 6,200,000 tons allowable production. He insisted that a capacity of 9,000,000 tons be maintained, since production does not normally reach 100 per cent of capacity. General Clay said that the United States would never agree to leaving Germany with a capacity higher than 8,000,000 tons or to reducing production below 6,000,000 tons. In general, Clay acted as a mediator between the extreme Russian and British views, and the French General Koeltz was willing to accept the American figures.

Complete agreement was not reached at this meeting. The delegates left, some of them to see whether they could get new instructions from their Governments. A second session brought agreement on the figure of 5,800,000 tons of annual production, but the Russians and the western Allies were separated by a mere 300,000 tons on the figure for allowable capacity. The matter was referred to the Control Council, where Sokolovsky (who was deputizing for Zhukov) made a concession by accepting the figure of 7,500,000 tons capacity, the lowest to which the other three would agree. This sounded like the happy ending. Compliments were passed about freely, Sokolovsky thanking Clay for his strenuous and skilful efforts to achieve agreement in the Co-ordinating Committee, and Montgomery (who was chairman that month) expressing his gratitude to Sokolovsky for his attitude, and on behalf of the Control Council thanking the Co-ordinating Committee for its efforts.

But all was not well. The next day the British received what they call a "rocket" from London. They were told they had made too many concessions. General Robertson was put in the embarrassing position of having to try to get a higher steel production without seeming to back down on the agreement. His formula was that the 5,800,000 figure was not necessarily the one that should be written into the economic plan and used as a basis for determining the level of other industries. He said that when the British agreed to the 7,500,000 figure for steel capacity they meant a capacity capable of actually producing that figure. The other delegations had obviously meant that 7,500,000 was the capacity that should be left in order to make possible an actual production of 5,800,000.

Logically the British position seemed indefensible, and even General Robertson, who is a master of the English language and is unsurpassed at lucid and persuasive exposition, was hard put to it to find convincing arguments. He said the British held hard to the condition laid down at Potsdam that it was a purpose of the occupation of Germany that the Allies should prepare for the eventual reconstruction of German political life on a democratic basis and for eventual peaceful co-operation in international life by Germany. He said the British believed that depressing the standard of living in Germany below a certain point would inevitably have an adverse effect on the economy of the rest of Europe and, indeed, of the world. He said the British delegation would never agree to converting Germany into a wilderness, and that they knew that no overall plan could be produced on the basis of 5,800,000 tons annual production without turning Germany into a wilderness. All this sounded perfectly reasonable, except that the British had previously accepted an annual production of 5,800,000 tons.

This deadlock was eventually by-passed when the Economics Directorate adopted a different approach and worked out the level of other industries without basing them on any particular steel production. Another ten weeks of negotiations similar to those described above were needed before agreement was reached on the plan as a whole. In the final discussions Clay again adopted the rôle of mediator, and it is doubtful whether there could have been any agreement at all without his efforts.

The objections he had to overcome were not all based on the necessity for depriving Germany of a war potential. For instance, nobody would argue that cement constitutes a war potential, and anyone would concede that Germany's need for cement in the next twenty years will be practically unlimited. Yet the French and Russians opposed leaving Germany with a cement capacity exceeding that of other European countries. General Koeltz argued that this would allow Germany to undertake building works in the reconstruction of the country faster than could other European nations. When the French held out for a drastic reduction in pharmaceuticals and dyestuffs, Clay said pointedly that he could not agree that they constituted a war potential, though he admitted that they might become the subject of commercial competition. This produced the desired effect, and Koeltz backed down, after assuring his colleagues that France had been exclusively guided by considerations of security and in no way by any commercial considerations.

In the background of all these negotiations one may see the tug of war between what are popularly referred to as the hard and soft peace schools. The expression is a convenient but a confusing one. There is no more virtue in being hard on the Germans because they unleashed the war and committed untold atrocities than there is in being soft on them because one feels sorry for them. The guilty should be punished to the greatest extent possible. The tragedy of it is that there is no way of punishing those most guilty adequately for the monstrous crimes they committed. One regrets that they have but one life to give for their crimes. How cheaply did a Hitler or a Himmler or a Goering pay for the millions of cruel deaths for which he was responsible! As for the average German who protested that he was "just a little man", his sufferings will be sufficient under the best of conditions to atone for his support of the Nazi war.

The Allied statesmen have proclaimed that vengeance should not be our policy. True statesmanship can have but one aim: to fashion a peace not hard, not soft, but sensible and enduring. The British proposals came nearest to meeting this criterion. The British deserve to be applauded for their efforts to find a way of disarming Germany effectively without ruining its economy. It would have been simple at a time when the passions engendered by war had not had time to abate, and when the memories of wrongs inflicted by the Germans were still fresh, to have followed a policy of hate.

America suffered far less at the hands of Germany than did Britain. Yet there were many more voices in America raised in support of the most fantastic plans for wrecking the German economy. American economic experts in Berlin studied the needs and possibilities of Germany's economy and had a pretty good idea of how far one could go in removing German productive capacity without crippling the country. A staff of these experts, under the direction of Dr. Calvin Hoover, made a careful study for General Clay with a view to determining a level of industry which would meet the Potsdam stipulations.

Dr. Hoover reported:

"The conclusion cannot be avoided that the conflict between an extreme degree of industrial disarmament spread

81

over a number of key industries and the goal of maintaining a minimum German standard of living according to the assumed formula while providing for the costs of the occupying forces seems insoluble under conditions such as those brought about by losses of territory. This is not to say that disarmament and the maintenance of a minimum civil economy are certainly mutually exclusive. It is possible that adequate industrial disarmament and a tolerable minimum standard of living could both be attained, if adequate control measures were continued in effect. The consideration of such control measures is, however, outside the scope of this report. Under the circumstances the decision as to how far the standard of living must be sacrificed in order to allow for necessary industrial disarmament is a decision which must be made in the realm of high policy."

General Clay read this report, and was very well aware of the problem. Had there been no other considerations involved he would very likely have come closer to sharing the British view. However, America is a democracy, and Clay had to be sensitive to trends of public opinion. He felt obliged to steer a middle course between the one recommended by the people who would deal most severely with Germany and those who would treat it most leniently. When he said America would not support a steel capacity in Germany greater than 8,000,000 tons or a production smaller than 6,000,000, that was his appraisal of the temper of public opinion at home. He was also motivated by a desire to reach agreement, and thereby increase the chances for the success of quadripartite government. This explains why he not only made concessions from the original American position, but even acted as mediator and conciliator between the other three.

The French estimates were lower than the Americans', partly because, being neighbours of Germany, they had more reason to fear her either as an independent aggressor or as a possible puppet of Russia. Another motive was undoubtedly the desire of French exporters to replace the Germans on world markets.

The Russians also feared German heavy industry, and were concerned lest it be turned against them by the British. If Sokolovsky's statement that 9,000,000 tons steel capacity would produce war in a few years meant anything, it meant that. Moreover, it is hard to over-estimate the effects of the desire for reparations of both the Russians and the French. Their countries had been invaded and their losses in property had been high. It was understandable that they should want to make the Germans pay as much as possible. They would not have been impressed by any suggestion that it is impossible to make a defeated and devastated country pay for the damage it has caused. Both the Russians and the French have frequently expressed amazement and chagrin at what they regarded as attempts by their Allies to deprive them of their just payment.

The Russians seem to have changed their minds lately about what is the best method of getting reparations from Germany. They have been reported as being willing to see the figure for permissible steel production doubled, meaning a rise to over 11,000,000 tons, provided they are given a direct voice in control of the Ruhr, and provided the increased production, or a large part of it, goes for reparations. The most likely explanation is that they believe, on the basis of recent experience, that they can get more out of Germany in the form of current production than by removals of installations.

It is natural that there should be differences of opinion about the extent to which it is necessary to sacrifice the German standard of living in the interests of security. To those who oppose a Carthaginian peace for Germany, self-styled hard peace advocates will answer: "Well, we haven't had any trouble from Carthage lately." The Romans razed Carthage to the ground and sowed salt on the site; and that was the end of the Carthaginian wars. But it was not the end of wars. The Allies might deal in similar manner with Germany, and there might never again be another German war. But that would not necessarily be the end of wars, either.

Americans who favour dealing drastically with Germany may be presumed not to be influenced by a desire for reparations. Most of them would also claim, as does Henry Morgenthau, Jr., not to be motivated by the much-publicized Morgenthau Plan, which is outlined in Morgenthau's book, "Germany is Our Problem", a book that offers no real solution to that problem. It is even a euphonism to call this collection of impractical ideas a plan. The very suggestion in the title of the book—that America should be concerned with Germany's future—is belied by the author's statement that "under this programme United States troops could be withdrawn within a relatively short time".

This is a scarcely veiled appeal to isolationist sentiment. Although he is not saying it in so many words, Mr. Morgenthau is in effect arguing: Let us reduce the German economy to chaos, and then Germany will be so impotent that Americans can safely withdraw. This would be much simpler than staying in Germany and helping to impose effective controls on a working German economy; but it would also be an evasion of our responsibilities. It is true that Mr. Morgenthau adds that the United States would "have full military and civilian representation on whatever international commission or commissions may be established for the execution of the whole German programme". Yet no realist would imagine that America's voice would carry much weight on such a commission unless it were backed up by armed force on the spot.

The Morgenthau "Plan" proposes to split Germany into a North German and South German State. The latter would include Bavaria, Wuerttemberg and Baden and some other small areas. The former would comprise what is now the Soviet zone plus a small part of the present British zone and some of the territory that was detached from Germany by the Potsdam Agreement and placed under Polish administration. East Prussia and Silesia, a small part of the Rhineland, and Schleswig-Holstein would be detached from Germany and given to the Soviet Union and Poland, France and Denmark. All that part of western Germany north of the Main and Moselle rivers and west of the Weser, but also including the Elbe estuary and the Kiel Canal, would also be detached and made an international zone.

In this zone Morgenthau proposes "all industrial plants and equipment not destroyed by military action shall be completely dismantled and transported to Allied Nations as restitutions. All equipment shall be removed from the mines and the mines closed." The plan is not consistent within itself because when the author takes up the problem of the Ruhr in detail he goes back on this idea of closing the Ruhr mines, and says the coal of the Ruhr should be used "for the benefit of European reconstruction and development generally". All the German miners should be replaced by French, Belgian, Dutch and other workers. The German population of the Ruhr area would be resettled in other parts of Germany.

Mr. Morgenthau does not make it quite clear whether he proposes to transfer the population of his entire international zone, or merely of the immediate Ruhr area. Even if only the latter is intended, there are several objections. The principle of mass transfers of populations, popularized by the Nazis themselves, seems to have been generally accepted in the post-war world. Even admitting that this is practicable and desirable, there is still the question of whether enough foreign workers could be found to resettle the area. Every country to-day is experiencing the greatest difficulty in finding enough coal-miners to work its own mines. This is true in England and France as well as in Germany. In Holland there is no body of trained coal-miners. France with its stationary and aging population would hardly be in a position to send several million people to settle in the Ruhr.

Furthermore, while it is possible to evict forcibly millions of defeated enemy nationals from their homes, the same measures could not be applied to citizens of Allied nations. Frenchmen like to live in France, and it is my guess that very few of them would be found ready to leave "la belle France" to settle down in an internationalized area of Germany. The same would probably hold true of Belgians and Dutchmen. The example of Poland, which has been unable to resettle the farms and cities from which it has ejected Germans, is instructive.

Even were it possible to fill the void left by Germans to be expelled from the Ruhr, there is the problem of where to put the expellees. Mr. Morgenthau suggests settling them on farms in the rump German States. He believes 5,000,000 workers and their families could be turned into farmers and could gain their livelihood on the land. This idea of turning Germany into an agricultural country, popularly known as the "goat-pasture economy" is the theme-song of the Morgenthau Plan. He believes the Germans, traditionally importers of food, could maximize and intensify agriculture to the point where they could not only feed themselves, but could even export the food necessary to pay for imports of fertilizers.

At the same time he advocates depriving them of some of their best food-producing areas (though not as much as they lost at Potsdam). Yet even if 5,000,000 workers could be absorbed on the reduced acreage of arable land, the problem would not be solved. Mr. Morgenthau favours transplanting not only the entire population of the Ruhr, but also workers who would be unemployed as a result of the dismantling of industries throughout Germany, as well as the German populations of East Prussia, Silesia and the other regions ceded by Germany. The extent of his error in arithmetic may be measured in part by his estimate of the post-war population of Germany, which he puts at between 55,000,000 and 60,000,000. The preliminary census of December, 1945, showed a population of 65,285,900 prior to the acceptance of over 6,000,000 expellees and an unknown number of prisoners of war.

Mr. Morgenthau was attracted by the idea that with German industry crippled, the United States could move in and supply European countries with the products they normally imported from Germany. Such considerations might well appeal to American exporters, but in any plan for world peace the prosperity of the international community should take precedence over the interests of any particular group in the United States or in any country. Its commercial imperialism as well as its political isolationism would be sufficient to throw grave suspicions on the Morgenthau "Plan", though this is almost incidental, since its main 'provisions are so obviously unrealistic and unworkable.

The extreme aspects of the Morgenthau Plan precluded its adoption by our Government. There was, however, a bitter fight during the early days of the occupation between representatives in Germany of the so-called hard and soft peace philosophies. The Treasury Department as well as the War and State Departments contributed personnel to the military government (thereby further complicating a situation already confused by divided allegiances). Men like Colonel Bernard Bernstein and Mr. Russell Nixon, popularly known as "Morgenthau boys", retained their posts long after their chief had left the government. The weight of their influence was thrown into the scales to balance American policy in the Morgenthau direction.

Late in 1945 there were 140 Treasury Department specialists in important military government jobs in Germany. In addition to their official duties, they acted as a kind of unofficial intelligence service for the department, and did considerable press-agenting for the Morgenthau view, particularly by "planting" stories with Press correspondents. But the Treasury Department lost out in its attempt to secure the right to name executives and advisors in the finance and external assets control branches of military government. The resignations of Bernstein and Nixon in November, 1945, over the issue of "getting tough" with neutral countries where German external assets were located, marked the end of the Treasury Department's excursion into the field of foreign affairs.

Paradoxically, the Morgenthau line was widely regarded as liberal, leftist and New Deal. It was actually negative and non-constructive. It advocated mass deportations of populations. It favoured the destruction of productive capacity, which meant lower living standards in and outside Germany. If carried out, it would have fostered among the Germans hate for the Allies and democracy, and kept alive feelings of violent nationalism to be exploited at the first opportunity by some new reactionary demagogue, some neo-Nazi. A truly liberal programme would have had to consider the problem of the moral and mental rehabilitation of the Germans and of an economic rehabilitation that would prevent Germany from being turned into a "wilderness", an economic sore that would infect the rest of Europe.

To impoverish Germany would lower the standard of living in surrounding countries because the European economy is a complicated, integrated mechanism, and Germany is an important part of that mechanism. Most of Europe's trade routes pass through Germany, so that it is in the interests of other countries that Germany's transportation system be restored. This cannot be done unless Germany is able to produce steel, locomotives, rolling stock, rails, barges and all kinds of other equipment.

Germany as a market is important to its neighbours. The effects of Germany's inability to buy are already making themselves felt on other national economies. The port of Rotterdam, to give one example, has been virtually stagnant since the war because of the loss of the German trade.

Germany normally supplies hundreds of products needed by other European nations. A number of these countries have been clamouring for spare parts and replacements for German-made machines. In 1939 and 1940, chemical products, machinery, mining products, textiles, steel, pig iron and finished metal goods accounted for over 75 per cent of Germany's exports.

It is conceivable that Germany's former customers might find other sources for these products, if Germany is no longer able to supply them. These customers would also have to find markets for the products they formerly sold to Germany, since they, too, must export if they are to import. The United States

87

might be willing to sell Denmark the agricultural machinery it formerly got from Germany; but the United States would hardly be likely to buy the Danish butter and eggs that Germany bought.

Looking at the problem as a general European or even world problem, it is clear that general living standards will be higher if each nation produces what it can make most economically. Germany's resources and geographical position enable it to manufacture the products it normally exports more cheaply than could the countries which bought these exports, and probably more cheaply than these countries could buy them elsewhere.

It would be uneconomical for Germany to try to become a primarily agricultural country, because there are other countries better favoured by nature for agriculture, and they can produce the food more cheaply. To state the problem in very simple terms, if agriculture is artificially encouraged in Germany, and if industry is artificially stimulated in countries lacking power sources and raw materials, less will be produced all round, and living standards will go down everywhere.

It is clear to anyone who has been in Germany that the "hard peace" advocates are influenced largely by their personal dislike for the Germans. It is easy to dislike or hate the Germans. The North Germans in particular are what the French call *pas sympathiques*. They get on one's nerves. They tend to be arrogant or fawning and self-pitying by turns, depending on whether or not they have the upper hand. I once heard an American friend of mine in Berlin, who is not a Germanophobe, tell another friend, who hates all Germans: "About four times a day I have to agree with you."

Yet neither blind hate nor a milder emotional antipathy, such as almost any American is bound to feel recurrently if he lives in Germany, will solve the problem, any more than will pity, which some other Americans have been inclined to feel for the Germans. It is necessary to be guided not by emotions but by such considerations as justice, security, sound economics, political common sense, and a broader humanitarianism —not pity, but a kind of *noblesse oblige*, which restrains us from committing crimes against humanity merely because others have done so, from violating our own principles of democracy and respect for human values, even when dealing with those who have not learned to value these principles.

88

In many respects the Potsdam plan violated these considerations. Its interpretation in the level of industry agreement or compromise did not make economic sense. All that can be said is that it was less unreasonable than the Morgenthau scheme. For instance, instead of closing down the coal mines, the Allies decided to maximize coal production so as to obtain the greatest possible coal exports. This would serve the double purpose of supporting the European economy and providing the means of paying for necessary imports. But other features of the level of industry plan were less sensible.

This may be illustrated by a comparison of the plan with the Hoover report, the technical study by experts mentioned above. Dr. Hoover interpreted the ambiguous Potsdam phrase "standard of living not exceeding the average of that in other European countries" as meaning a standard equal to that average. He found that in order to meet this average, the average German standard of living for the years from 1930 to 1938 would have to be reduced to about 74 per cent, or to approximately the level of the depression year, 1932, in Germany. In order to cut down on imports he recommended a diet that would be lower in calories than the 1932 diet and would be poorer because it would contain less fats, oils and meats. The actual calorie level he set was 2,600 a day (compared with about 3,200 in the United States). He calculated that losses of territory had deprived Germany of 25 per cent of its arable land and that food imports to the amount of 2,300,000,000 reichsmarks would be needed to support his recommended diet. To this he added 1,900,000,000 reichsmarks of other imports he considered necessary.

He then looked around for means of producing exports to balance these imports. Because of the need for eliminating war potential industries, and reducing the capacity in industries that were not primarily war industries but might be of primary importance in war-time, his exports fell short of his imports by over 200,000,000 marks (without counting costs of occupation). The following table gives key figures for the German economy in 1936, as recommended in the Hoover report; and as finally adopted by the Control Council in the level of industry plan (using the year 1949 as the one when the German economy might be expected to recover to the permitted level).

	1936.	*Hoover.*	1949 (*A.C.C.*).
Population (millions) . .	69·6 (1939)	70·0	66·5
Exports (RM. millions) . .	4,768	3,967	3,000
Imports (RM. millions) .	4,218	4,200	3,000
Food Imports (RM. millions) .	1,499	2,300	1,500
Food Consumption (calories per person per day) . . .	2,900 (1930–38 average)	2,600	2,500–2,700
Steel Ingots (million tons) .	19·2	7·8	5·8
Electric Power (millions of KW. installed capacity) . .	15·2	11·0	9·0
Passenger Cars and Light Trucks	304,000	100,000	80,000

The year 1936 is good for comparative purposes for several reasons. It was not a year of extreme economic depression or prosperity. Rearmament had not gone far enough to account for more than a small proportion of production. On the other hand, the Nazis were already exerting strenuous efforts to make Germany self-sufficient. Thus one gets a good idea of what could be done in the way of drastic reduction of imports. Food imports, for instance, were lower in 1936 than in any previous or subsequent year. The Hoover report estimates a higher requirement because of the losses of productive land which were not offset by a reduction in population. The Control Council was able to reduce this figure again, partly because it assumed a smaller population (which was almost certainly unrealistic), and partly because it was more optimistic about the amount of food that could be obtained from indigenous resources. Both the Hoover report and the level of industry plan are equated to 1936 prices. The 1939 population is exclusive of Austria and the Sudetenland. The other population estimates are based on the present boundaries of Germany (including the Saar) after expellees have been absorbed. They assume that there will be no natural population increase by 1949.

The following table gives the capacities of other basic industries permitted in the level of industry plan, expressed in percentages of pre-war production (in some instances, 1936, in others, 1938):—

Machine tools	.	.	.	.	11·4
Heavy engineering	.	.	.	31
Light engineering	.	.	.	50
Electrical engineering	.	.	50
Precision instruments and optics	.	70
Basic chemicals	.	.	.	40
Pharmaceuticals	.	.	.	80
Cement	.	.	.	.	68
Tractors	.	.	.	.	72
Other agricultural machinery	.	80
Paper	.	.	.	.	65
Boots and shoes	.	.	.	70
Textiles	.	.	.	.	77

Industries which were to be completely eliminated by the removal of all industrial equipment included, in addition to armaments and munitions, aircraft and sea-going ships:—

Synthetic gasoline and oil.
Synthetic rubber.
Synthetic ammonia.
Ball and taper roller bearings.
Heavy machine tools of certain types.
Heavy tractors.
Primary aluminium.
Magnesium.
Beryllium.
Vanadium produced from Thoas Slags.
Radio-active materials.
Hydrogen peroxide above 50% strength.
Specific war chemicals and gases.
Radio transmitting equipment.

Exceptions were foreseen in the case of synthetic gasoline and oil, synthetic rubber, synthetic ammonia, and ball and taper roller bearings, for which capacity was to be temporarily retained until imports to meet domestic requirements were available and could be paid for.

General Robertson said at a Press conference given after the plan was announced that he believed it would leave sufficient capacity in the mining and manufacturing industries (exclusive of building and building materials) to produce at approximately 50 to 55 per cent of the 1938 level. Having agreed to the plan, he could not very well criticize it, even though the correspondents knew that he himself believed it cut German industry too drastically, that he had subscribed to it only in the interests of quadripartite agreement, and that he was personally sceptical about its workability. This scepticism he cautiously expressed by saying:

"I would remind you that this plan has been drawn up in accordance with the principles laid down at Potsdam in the Berlin Protocol. This alone postulates the fact that the Plan is a very drastic one. It will not be easy for Germany to recover under this Plan even up to the economic standard permitted by the Plan. The Germans are being set a very hard task. One should not, however, forget that the Germans possess an amazing power of recovery. Anybody who fought against them during the war knows but too well that this is so. If the skill and organizing power of the German people are developed not to war but to overcoming their economic difficulties we believe that sufficient productive resources have been left to them to enable them to obtain a tolerable living standard in line with the European average. I say we believe this, but I cannot say categorically that it will be so. *There is no margin of safety* to counteract any unforeseen political or economic developments which may occur within or without the frontiers of Germany to disturb the rehabilitation of the country."

His suggestion that the plan itself would make it difficult for the Germans to recover to the level permitted by the plan is particularly significant. The very drastic reduction in machine-tool capacity would be sufficient in itself to raise grave doubts as to the extent to which the Germans would be able to maintain and replace their aging machines, overworked during six years of war. The Allies agreed that the older and less efficient plants would be left in Germany, while the best ones would be removed as reparations. A more open criticism of the plan was given in *The Economist* of London in an article that appeared in the issue of April 6, 1946:—

"On the threshold of industrial history [*The Economist* wrote] the workers sought to end their misery by smashing the machines which appeared to have created it. To-day, in the plan for reparations and the level of post-war German economy there is more than a trace of the same spirit. The Allies are in fact proposing an unparalleled essay in international machine wrecking. The attitude is understandable. The Nazis have caused misery enough to make the desire to smash their machine attractive to millions of dispossessed Europeans. But this does not alter the fact that the mood reflected in the Allied plan for German industry is as anachronistic and dangerous as the primitive and spontaneous machine-smashing of the Luddite age.

"Criticism of the plan does not apply primarily to this or that set of its specific provisions, but to the economic philosophy that inspires it, the philosophy of rigid economic restrictionism."

Analysing the plan, *The Economist* concluded that it would give Germany a national income not equal to the average European level, but about one-third below the European average in 1938. The British periodical pointed out that "agricultural and peaceful industries" cannot develop without a sufficient supply of capital goods for replacement and expansion; that the planned bottle-necks in machine-tools and steel would strangle Germany's other industries, preventing them from achieving even the permitted quotas; and that production planned on the level of the Great Depression would produce a standard of living lower than the depression level because during the depression each nation consumed accumulated stocks, and such stocks do not exist in Germany.

The Economist then proposed an alternative solution to the problem of controlling Germany's war potential without drastically reducing its standard of living:

"It is possible to ensure against German rearmament without driving Germany into starvation and unemployment. The method should be to impose no restrictions on industrial processes and to call a halt to the stripping of German industry, but to prohibit absolutely the manufacture of certain easily recognizable industrial end-products. If the manufacture of armaments is effectively prohibited, then the restriction of industrial processes need not be. And if the manufacture of armaments cannot be effectively prohibited, then the far more cumbrous and elaborate industrial prohibitions certainly will not be.

"This policy stands no chance of acceptance now, but its

93

later acceptance is more likely in that it could be worked out through a modification, rather than the complete repeal, of the Potsdam plan—provided it happens quickly enough. If the change of mind comes before Germany is completely stripped and impoverished, then it could be effected merely by pruning the list of prohibited industries and cancelling the list of restrictions.

"Nor need this lead to any reduction in reparations, for there is no reason why German industry should not work, for ten years, to rebuild and re-equip the ravished victors—provided that a term is set to the penal period. What is so defeatist and self-defeating about the present policy is that it holds out no hope either to the Germans of ever purging their guilt and bettering their condition or to the occupying powers of ever being relieved of the very heavy burden of repressing and administering the Germans.

"The present policy, in fact, is a vicious circle. The more it impoverishes the Germans, the more surely unregenerate it makes them, the more difficult it makes the complete devastation of Germany as a means of defence. But the spiral could work upwards. The more hope is held out to the Germans, the more ready they would be to accept the conditions on which it is offered, the safer it would be to relax their conditions of life, and the more hope could be held out to them."

At the time it subscribed to the level of industry plan, His Majesty's Government issued a statement to the effect that it could be accepted only if certain basic assumptions on which it was founded were proved to be correct. These assumptions were: (1) that Germany, with its present western frontiers remaining unchanged, would be treated as a single economic unit; (2) that the population of Germany would not exceed 66,500,000; and (3) that markets could be found for the exports envisaged in the plan as necessary to pay for the required imports. If one or more of these assumptions were proved incorrect, said H.M. Government, the plan would have to be revised.

It has already been suggested that the second assumption—of a population of only 66,500,000—is not correct. With regard to the first assumption, if the Saar, for instance, were detached from Germany and annexed by France, this could be com-

94

pensated for by allowing a higher production in the Ruhr. But if Germany is not treated as an economic unit (and eighteen months after the end of the war little progress has been made in this direction), the plan would not only have to be revised, but completely scrapped. The third assumption is likewise open to question. In order to compensate for the loss of exports from prohibited or restricted industries it was necessary to provide for increased exports in the "peaceful domestic industries". The capacity of foreign markets to absorb textiles, ceramics, toys, bicycles, aspirin tablets, etc., after 1949 is hard to estimate, but it will not be without limits (though the market for aspirin ought to be good).

There were many observers in Germany who doubted whether the four occupation Powers would ever be able to reconcile their sharply differing views sufficiently to agree on a level of industry for Germany. Agreement was finally achieved because all parties were willing to make concessions. None of the four was willing to let the quadripartite machinery break down at that time and over that issue. Moreover, the Russians and French were anxious to start collecting their reparations, and accepted compromises to which they might not have agreed if the question of the future level of the German economy had not been linked to that of reparations. But in view of the doubtful wisdom of its more drastic provisions and the shakiness of the assumptions upon which it is based, about the best one can say of the level of industry agreement is that it was an agreement.

VI

AMERICA'S GERMAN POLICY

NEWS PICTURE

THE two documents from which I have reproduced extracts below were the first clear public statements of Soviet and American policy in Germany. They have been widely discussed and have been the subject of acrimonious debates by numerous columnists and commentators.

A. MOLOTOV IN PARIS, JULY 10, 1946.

"The time has come when we should discuss the fate of Germany and a peace treaty with that country.

"The Soviet Government has always held that the spirit of revenge is a poor counselor in such affairs. It would be incorrect to identify Hitler Germany with the German people, though the German people cannot divest themselves of the responsibility for Germany's aggression and for its gravest consequences.

"I proceed from the fact that in the light of the interests of the world economy and tranquility in Europe it would be incorrect to adopt a course of Germany's annihilation as a state or that of its agrarianization including the annihilation of its main industrial centers.

"Such a course would result in undermining the economy of Europe, in the dislocation of world economy and in a chronic political crisis in Germany which would spell a threat to peace and tranquility.

"Germany has long held an important position in the world economy. While continuing as a single State, Germany will remain an important factor in world trade. This also corresponds to the interests of other peoples. On the other hand, a policy of annihilation of Germany as a State or of its agrarianization and annihilation of its principal industrial centers would result in making Germany a center where dangerous sentiments of revenge would be nourished and would play into the hands of German reactionaries and deprive Europe of tranquility and a stable peace.

"It has of late become fashionable to talk about the dismemberment of Germany into several autonomous States, about the federalization of Germany and about the separation of the Ruhr from Germany. All such proposals originate in the same policy of destruction and agrarianization

96

of Germany, for it is easy to understand that without the Ruhr, Germany cannot exist as an independent and viable State. But I have already said that if the interests of peace and tranquility are dear to us the destruction of Germany should not be our objective. . . .

"In order that the development of German peaceful industries may be of benefit to other peoples who need German coal, metals and manufactured products, Germany should be granted the right to export and import, and if this right of foreign trade is to be implemented we should not put obstacles in the way of an increase in the output of steel, coal and manufactured products of a peaceful nature in Germany, naturally within certain bounds and provided that an inter-allied control is established over German industry, and over the Ruhr industries in particular.

"As we know, the Control Council in Germany recently fixed the level which would be reached by German industries in the near future. Germany has not yet by far reached this level. Nevertheless, it should already now be admitted that peaceful industries in Germany must be given an opportunity to develop on a wider scale provided only that this industrial development is really used to satisfy the peaceful needs of the German people and the requirements of trade with other countries. . . ."

B. BYRNES IN STUTTGART, SEPT. 6, 1946.

"The United States is firmly of the belief that Germany should be administered as an economic unit and that zonal barriers should be completely obliterated so far as the economic life and activity in Germany are concerned.

"Important as economic unification is for the recovery of Germany and of Europe, the German people must recognize that the basic cause of their suffering and distress is the war which the Nazi dictatorship brought upon the world.

"But just because suffering and distress in Germany are inevitable, the American Government is unwilling to accept responsibility for the needless aggravation of economic distress that is caused by the failure of the Allied Control Council to agree to give the German people a chance to solve some of their most urgent economic problems.

"It is the view of the American Government that the German people, throughout Germany, under proper safeguards, should now be given the primary responsibility for the running of their own affairs.

"More than a year has passed since hostilities ceased. The millions of German people should not be forced to live in doubt as to their fate. It is the view of the American Government that the Allies without delay should make clear to the German people the essential terms of the peace settlement which they expect the German people to accept and observe.

D (Struggle for Germany)

It is our view that the German people should now be permitted and helped to make the necessary preparations for the setting up of a democratic German government which can accept and observe those terms.

"All that the Allied Governments can and should do is to lay down the rules under which German democracy can govern itself. Allied occupation forces should be limited to a number sufficient to see that those rules are obeyed.

"Security forces will probably have to remain in Germany for a long period. I want no misunderstanding. We will not shirk our duty. We are not withdrawing. As long as an occupation force is required in Germany, the American Army will furnish its proportionate share of that force.

"The time has also come to define the boundaries of the new Germany.

"The heads of Government agreed to support at the peace settlement the proposal of the Soviet Government concerning the ultimate transfer to the Soviet Union of the City of Koenigsberg and the area adjacent to it. Unless the Soviet Government changes its views on the subject, we will certainly stand by our agreement.

"The Soviets and the Poles suffered greatly at the hands of Hitler's invading armies. As a result of an agreement at Yalta, Poland ceded to the Soviet Union territory east of the Curzon Line. Because of this, Poland asked for a revision of her northern and western frontiers. The United States will support a revision of these frontiers in Poland's favor. However, the extent of the area to be ceded to Poland must be determined when the final settlement is agreed upon.

"The United States does not feel that it can deny to France, which has been invaded three times by Germany in seventy years, its claim to the Saar territory, whose economy has long been closely linked with France. Of course, if the Saar territory is integrated with France, she should readjust her reparation claims against Germany.

"Except as here indicated, the United States will not support any encroachment on territory which is indisputably German, or any division of Germany which is not genuinely desired by the people concerned. So far as the United States is aware, the people of the Ruhr and the Rhineland desire to remain united with the rest of Germany. And the United States will not oppose their desire.

"The United States will favor such controls over the whole of Germany, including the Ruhr and Rhineland, as may be necessary for security purposes. It will help to enforce those controls. But it will not favor any controls that would subject the Ruhr and Rhineland to political domination or manipulation of outside powers.

"The German people are now feeling the devastating effects of the war which Hitler and his minions brought upon the world. Other people felt *those devastating effects long before they were brought home to the German people.*

"The United States cannot relieve Germany from the hardships inflicted upon her by the war her leaders started. But the United States has no desire to increase those hardships or to deny the German people an opportunity to work their way out of those hardships so long as they respect human freedom and follow the paths of peace.

"The American people want to return the Government of Germany to the German people. The American people want to help the German people to win their way back to an honorable place among the free and peace-loving nations of the world."

MANY Americans are convinced that the Russian, British and French Governments and their representatives act consistently in accordance with a carefully worked out, and probably somewhat sinister, plan. Their own Government they presume to be guided by a kind of misty idealism which renders it an easy prey to the devilish and self-interested machinations of the others. This belief may be behind the queries so frequently heard during the first year of the occupation as to why we have no policy in Germany.

I once had occasion to call this criticism to the attention of General Clay, whose job it is to administer American policy in Germany. The General, who is a reasonably self-contained man, waxed indignant. He launched into a long exposition of American aims and policy. What he said can be summarized in five words: Denazification, Demilitarization, Decentralization, Deindustrialization—and Democratization. The negative prefix to the first four of these linguistic atrocities suggests clearly enough the amount of tearing down we felt to be necessary around Germany before we could advance to the more constructive process implied in the fifth. Together these five "D's" of the occupation symbolized the American conception of how to implement the basic policy of preventing Germany from ever again becoming a menace to world peace.

General Clay's displeasure with the "Why don't we have any policy in Germany?" type of criticism came from his awareness that the United States had taken the initiative in trying to make this policy a reality. In their own zone the Americans had gone farther than any of their Allies in denazifying, demilitarizing, decentralizing, politically, and deindustrializing both by destroying war potential plants and

99

by breaking up cartels. At four-Power meetings the Americans had pressed for uniform action in these fields. Of course mistakes were made, and sometimes important things were left undone for a long time. Legitimate criticisms could be directed at the way our policy had been carried out. That did not imply that we had none.

The suggestion implicit in the charge that we had no policy might have been that it was not enough to say what we intended to do with Germany, but that we must also define our policy towards our Allies and fit our German policy into our general foreign policy. About a year after the end of the war, Byrnes and Clay actually did take steps to fit our German policy into a foreign policy which was being shaped increasingly by the necessity for dealing with a two-world situation. Without rejecting a single United Nations world as a desirable consummation, the United States was more and more consciously assuming the rôle of leader of the Western world in opposition to the Eastern world.

Potsdam was the last of the secret conferences, where squabbling went on behind closed doors and the world was mercifully sheltered from the spectacle of Allied disunity. Beginning at the Conference of Foreign Ministers in London in September, 1945, the spectacle became a public one (and the disunity became more pronounced because the end of the war had ended the urgency of the need for unity). The procedural disagreements upon which this Conference broke up seemed trivial; they were symptomatic of a more basic cleavage.

Of the two European countries where Russians and Americans had to deal with one another continually, it was in Austria rather than in Germany that the issues dividing them were first clearly recognized and openly disputed. Austria was, in theory at least, a liberated country, and the benevolent American occupation need not have the same scruples in supporting the Austrians against the Russians as was the case in Germany. General Clark moved to Vienna (the capital and seat of the four-Power Control Council) to be on the scene of action (both Eisenhower and McNarney had their head-quarters in Frankfurt, not Berlin). Clark assumed with little reluctance the rôle of defender of Austrian independence against every Russian attempt to bring that small but centrally located, and therefore strategic, country into the Soviet orbit.

For the Americans in Germany to have a corresponding rôle

would hardly have been appropriate. Clay, in Berlin, did not want a knock-down, drag-out fight with the Russians. He conceived that it was wrong for the Allies to use the Germans or any German factions against each other. He believed that differences between the Allies should as far as possible be settled in private, and not aired to the German public. This was the official position of all the delegations, who agreed that their meetings should be closed to the Press and that only agreed decisions should be given publicity. As a newspaperman, I would have liked to witness these meetings. But I must admit that there was some merit in the arrangement. It was easier for negotiators to make concessions if the whole world did not know that they were backing down. Furthermore, the meetings of the Control Council were prevented from becoming forums for political and propaganda speeches, as happened at United Nations sessions, at the Foreign Ministers' conferences and at the Peace Conference. It is true that the Press was not invited to the "Big Four" meetings, but it was given play-by-play accounts—by members of the several delegations, each with an axe to grind.

Of course the Control Council secrecy could not succeed for long in concealing from the Germans that all was not well in the family of the occupation Powers. The German public was astute enough and practised enough at reading between the lines of official communications not to be deceived even if all the Allies had really tried to keep them in a state of blissful ignorance. The Allies did not try very hard; and the newspapers in the several sectors of Berlin became the vehicles for criticisms and attacks on the occupying Powers—attacks that became progressively less subtle.

Clay's original premise was that the Allies should stick to the letter and spirit of Potsdam and should co-operate loyally in carrying out their declared policy of converting Germany into a democratic, peace-loving nation that would not be a threat to the peace of the world. Whatever the faults of Potsdam, we had agreed to it, and should observe it as long as there was a chance that it could be carried out. If other nations failed to live up to Potsdam, the United States might have to reconsider its position, but America should not be the first to violate the agreement.

In line with this thinking, he made every effort to avoid sharpening the developing East–West cleavage. He did nothing to line up the three Western Powers against the Russians. On some issues he sided with the Russians and British against the French; on others with the Russians and French against the British. His personal relations with General Sokolovsky were excellent. He once told me: "I have voted with the Russians more often than with any other delegation." That was in the early days.

During the first year he frequently assumed the rôle of mediator between the other Powers, and with some success; while the United States element of the Control body, under his direction, took the initiative in introducing more papers for quadripartite action than any other delegation. American relations with the Russians were undoubtedly better in Berlin than anywhere else in the world; but the time came, approximately a year after VE-Day, when governmental disagreement on major issues practically blocked any further progress in the Control Council.

Readers may wonder how it came about that Clay, as Deputy Military Governor, implemented, and to a large degree shaped, American policy in Germany. Eisenhower had tended increasingly to let him take over the military government job; McNarney (who succeeded Eisenhower in November, 1945) deputized him with the full responsibility for military government. Thus Clay dealt directly with Washington, merely sending information copies of his communications to McNarney in Frankfurt. Even on high policy matters Clay often took action without reference to the War or State Departments. With the decline in the importance of the Control Council in relation to the Co-ordinating Committee, he also became the chief American spokesman in four-Power deliberations.

It was Clay who made the decision to hold the first elections in Germany since 1933 in the American zone. It was Clay, too, who took the responsibility for ordering a suspension of reparations removals from the United States zone on the grounds that the Potsdam decision to treat Germany as an economic whole must be carried out before the reparations clauses. In ways such as these, Clay shaped American policy within the broad framework of his directives, and within what he conceived to be the limits of toleration of American public opinion. Washington never failed to back him up. In one respect he was particularly fortunate because Secretary of State Byrnes had been his boss when Byrnes was Director of War

Mobilization and Reconversion and Clay was his Deputy for War Production. Byrnes' confidence and support were of great value to him.

During the spring and summer of 1946 the two men met several times in Paris and once in Berlin, and it was at these meetings that America's German policy was reconsidered and reshaped in view of the continued refusal of France to accept certain principles of Potsdam and the failure of Russia to live up to them. At the Foreign Ministers' Conference in Paris, Byrnes defended and re-affirmed Clay's reparations suspension as in line with American policy. The offer to one or more of the other zones to merge economically with the American zone was made at this time. A "hard peace" for Germany was formally and publicly rejected by Byrnes, and an early peace treaty and an end of "mass occupations" were demanded.

In September Byrnes took the unprecedented step of coming to Germany to address American-appointed German officials, as well as American military government officers, in Stuttgart. In his speech, written after consultation with Clay, Byrnes took a stand on every important issue related to the German problem. For the first time, American views on Germany's frontiers were clearly stated. We would support French claims to the Saar, but would oppose separation of the Ruhr and Rhineland from Germany unless the population concerned desired it (which it clearly did not). We would support Russian claims to the Koenigsberg region of East Prussia, as agreed at Potsdam, and the principle of extending Poland's frontiers to the west at Germany's expense in compensation for territory ceded to Russia; but we would not defend the extension of Poland to the Oder–Neisse line.

Our position on reparations was stated more precisely than ever before: the level of economy agreed on by the Control Council would not permit the exaction of reparations from current production. (Byrnes left open the possibility that he would agree to this form of reparations if the economic level were raised.) The creation of a provisional government for Germany was advocated. Byrnes spoke out in no doubtful terms on the question of a hard or soft peace:

"The American people want peace. They have long since ceased to talk of a hard or a soft peace for Germany. This never has been the real issue. What we want is a lasting peace. We will oppose harsh and vengeful measures which obstruct an effective peace. We will oppose soft measures which invite the breaking of the peace."

The Byrnes speech was the culmination of a year of development of America's German policy. It did not renounce Potsdam, but it went beyond Potsdam, clarifying the American attitude towards the issues that had been ignored or dodged at Potsdam. It has been criticized as a bid for the favour of the Germans, in answer to a previous bid by Molotov (in the statement quoted at the beginning of this chapter). But critics should consider what it was that Byrnes was offering the Germans. He was in effect telling them: our brand of democracy offers you a chance of economic recovery, eventually even prosperity. Unless this hope were held out to them the German democrats could never succeed in creating a democratic Germany.

Byrnes was at the same time defining for the Germans the American concept of democracy. Being pledged to assist in building a democratic Germany, we could hardly do less than tell the Germans what we meant by democracy and what kind of a life they might expect under it. Admittedly the Russians were preaching a different kind of democracy. Admittedly we were in an ideological conflict with them. We could not pretend indefinitely that we all meant the same thing when we spoke of democracy. Nor could we, if we really believed in our brand of democracy, refrain, even in the interests of Allied unity, from speaking up for it and campaigning for it. Many Americans may have believed at first that the Russians meant the same thing as we did when they spoke of democracy and agreed that Germany should be a democracy. If this had been a mistaken view, it was as well to recognize the fact and state it openly.

A weakness in Byrnes' argument was his suggestion that the principle of self-determination should be applied to the Ruhr and Rhineland. If it should apply there, why should it not apply to the Saar, to East Prussia and Silesia? There was no logical reason. But the United States could not very well back down on its commitment to let Russia annex the Koenigsberg area since we had given our official approval at Potsdam to this *fait accompli*. At Yalta we had agreed to compensate Poland from German lands for the areas it ceded to Russia. The

Atlantic Charter had been scrapped at Yalta and Potsdam, and it would have been better to have kept discreetly silent about the principle of self-determination. As for the Saar, Byrnes hoped by this concession to reach an accord with the French about the Ruhr and Rhineland.

The most significant thing of all about Byrnes' speech was the fact that it was made, where it was made, when it was made. For the first time an American statesman spoke frankly to the Germans about Germany, not hesitating to criticize the actions of America's allies, at least by implication. It was the signal that America's German policy had been finally formulated and integrated with its whole foreign policy, and that America was ready to speak out openly in support of its policy. The enlistment of support in Germany for our policy became an integral part of that policy.

This foreign policy was as aggressive as the Russians' in the sense that we were equally convinced of the superiority of our system, of our form of democracy, equally ready to crusade for it in all parts of the world. Our insistence (to the extent that we were in a position to insist) on the introduction of democratic processes and the holding of fair elections in Rumania and Poland may be considered the equivalent of the indirect influence exerted by Russia in France through the Communist party there.

This policy was developed after the end of the war to replace the Roosevelt policy of subordinating everything to the winning of the war. That our ideological crusade went hand in hand with expansion by the acquisition of far-flung bases seemed as hypocritical to the Russians as many of their actions did to us when we compared them with their words. In Germany, too, the ideological competition and the struggle for control were inextricably intertwined. And the focal point of this contest was Berlin, important as the traditional capital of Germany and as the place where the four occupying Powers were in daily contact with one another.

Clay had been quick to perceive the political importance of Berlin, and shortly after the Americans entered their occupation sector of the city he established his main headquarters there. In the summer of 1945 there was a curious duality between Berlin and Frankfurt, with each military government division having echelons in both cities. There were thus two capitals for the American zone, and the technical absurdity of this situation is easy to imagine. Telephone communications between Berlin and Frankfurt were worse than poor in the first months. A regular train service did not exist in those early days, and air travel was dependent on the weather. The trip by road took nine or ten hours. American officers from General Eisenhower downwards wasted days commuting between the two cities, and spent hours on the telephone, which was not secure in any case, and was therefore unsuitable for the discussion of secret or confidential matters.

Clay planned to make Berlin the sole capital of the American zone, to separate military government from direct Army control, and to civilianize it. (Eventually he himself hoped to retire in favour of a civilian governor.) In October, 1945, eight of the principal military government branches had their main headquarters moved to Berlin. Eight others were to have offices in both Berlin and Frankfurt, while only three would remain centred in Frankfurt, with advance echelons in Berlin. Even those remaining in Frankfurt would no longer be under the G-5 Division of Army Headquarters (U.S.F.E.T.), but would constitute the Office of Military Government (U.S. Zone). The final move to Berlin of all military government functions was delayed by the failure of the Allies, notably the French, to agree to central administrations for Germany. The move was made, nevertheless, in April, and Frankfurt ceased to be anything but a military headquarters.

The British and French made no parallel moves. The latter continued to run their zone from the delightful resort town of Baden-Baden on the edge of the Black Forest. The British headquarters were dispersed in half a dozen small, unbombed towns on the Westphalian plain—Minden, Herford, Bunde, Lubbecke, Bad Oeynhausen. (Visitors approaching one of the main British military government offices were generally taken aback by a road sign reading: "BAD BENDS . . . BAD SURFACE . . . BAD OEYNHAUSEN.") The Russians did not need to worry about duality of headquarters, since Berlin was an island in their zone; they concentrated everything at Karlshorst in the eastern part of Berlin.

With the eclipse of Frankfurt as a military government capital, a new political capital for the American zone grew up at Stuttgart. Clay had hoped to avoid doing anything to perpetuate the arbitrary and artificial zonal boundaries in Germany. But the failure to establish central German administra-

106

tive agencies and to obtain agreement on other measures necessary to achieve economic unity forced the crystallization of zonal frontiers as political and economic barriers. The Russians were the first to centralize their zone; as early as August, 1945, they set up twelve central departments headed by German State secretaries. Clay conceived of the future Germany as a federalized nation which would give a large measure of autonomy to States and provinces. This was his interpretation of the Potsdam directive for decentralization. In the old Reich, Prussia, with two-thirds of Germany's population, had dominated the more than twenty other small States and city-States. All functions of government were highly centralized in Berlin, as capital of Prussia and Germany: In any scheme for decentralizing Germany, first place would have to be given to ending the dominance of Prussia—in fact, to ending its existence as a political entity; its component provinces could be given an equivalent status to that of the smaller States, like Bavaria, Thuringia and Wuerttemberg; while the archaic city-States could be incorporated into the new States and provinces. There would be a minimum of centralization in Berlin—only as much as would be necessary to run Germany as an economic entity.

Clay saw no value in the kind of decentralization that was represented by the division of Germany into four zones. They had no economic or historical justification, and he believed authority should go directly from the capital to the States, as it does in the United States. The zonal system would correspond to splitting the United States into far western, western, southern and north-eastern zones. Clay wanted to lay the basis for this new German federalism in the American zone. Unfortunately the zonal barriers cut across State lines, and it was necessary to reshuffle the German geography a bit. Bavaria (except for the Palatinate) was entirely in the American zone and was a natural entity. The northern halves of Baden and Wuerttemberg lay in the American zone and the southern halves in the French zone. An expedient of necessity was to take these two northern halves and incorporate them as a State of Wuerttemberg-Baden. The rest of the zone—Hesse and bits of Prussia—were thrown together to form the third State, Greater Hesse.

Instead of creating a tight zonal authority over these States, Clay preferred to use the American zone for an experiment in federalism that might later be extended to the rest of Germany.

The minister presidents or prime ministers of the three newly created States became members of a Laenderrat or Council of States, whose job it would be to confer on matters requiring co-ordination between the States. States' rights would be observed to the maximum extent possible. But it was obvious that zonal co-ordination was necessary in all the fields where national co-ordination was held up. The Laenderrat had no legislative powers; but agreed decisions were implemented by each minister president in his State. Each of the three members of the Council enjoyed the veto right. It was never used as recklessly as it has been in more august bodies.

The Council met once monthly in Stuttgart. It was subordinated to a Military Government Regional Co-ordinating Office, headed by Clay's appointee, Dr. James Pollock, a professor of political science on leave from the University of Michigan. Pollock has been much criticized for giving the Germans too much self-government too early. It should, however, be observed that all decisions by the Laenderrat had to be approved by military government in order to become effective. Moreover, if the Germans were to be trained for democracy, it seemed only reasonable to give them experience, under proper controls, in the processes of democracy as understood by Americans.

In a country where the best democratic elements had been ruthlessly suppressed and to a large degree exterminated during twelve years of Nazi dictatorship, the greatest problem was to find suitable leaders. The men found were too old and the democratic forms they knew dated back to an era that could not be revived. The Weimar Republic had failed and was dead. A new democracy was needed, and it required new, young leaders. Until they could be developed from a reclaimed youth, the old leaders must do.

Despite these shortcomings Byrnes and Clay were satisfied enough with the performance of the Laenderrat to feel that it had justified their hopes that the kind of federalism it represented was adaptable to Germany as a whole. This therefore was the type of provisional government proposed by Byrnes in his Stuttgart speech.

He said:

"The United States favors the early establishment of a provisional German Government for Germany. Progress has been made in the American zone in developing local and state self-government in Germany, and the American Government believes that similar progress is possible in all zones.

"It is the view of the American Government that the provisional government should not be hand-picked by other governments but should be a German National Council composed of the democratically responsible Minister Presidents or other chief officials of the several states or provinces which have been established in each of the four zones.

"Subject to the reserved authority of the Allied Control Council, the German National Council should be responsible for the proper functioning of the central administrative agencies which should have adequate power to ensure the administration of Germany as an economic unit as was contemplated by the Potsdam Agreement.

"The German National Council should also be charged with the preparation of a draft of a federal constitution for Germany which among other things should ensure the democratic character of the new Germany and the human rights and fundamental freedoms of all its inhabitants.

"After approval in principle by the Allied Control Council, the proposed constitution should be submitted to the German people for ratification."

The Russians quarrel with this federalization plan on the ground that it amounts to splitting up Germany into autonomous states. Byrnes and Clay would deny this, and say that it is merely their method of implementing the Potsdam provision for decentralization. Some American critics—for instance, Mr. Walter Lippmann—do not believe it goes far enough in the direction of decentralization. Lippmann's view, as I understand it, is that Germany should be broken up into a number of sovereign States which could then join in a confederation if they so chose. This kind of eighteenth-century Jeffersonian democracy is practically inconceivable in a modern State, particularly an industrial one. The degree of Germany's federalization will bear a relationship to the degree of its de-industrialization. In any event, the developments of the nineteenth and twentieth centuries in transportation and communication make a considerable degree of centralization in administration essential.

The merit of the Clay–Byrnes proposal is that it would effectively eliminate the predominance of Prussia in Germany. The country will be politically healthier with component States of more nearly equal size. But to break Germany up into a number of small, sovereign States would be to turn the clock back. In the world of to-morrow, old frontiers must be broken down, not new ones created. The peace of the world will be served best, not by splitting Germany up and then confederating the parts, but by preparing it to fit into a world confederation.

VII

"I WANNA GO HOME"

NEWS PICTURE

. . . CLAY SEES GERMANY RULED FOR GENERATION SAYS OCCUPA-
TION WILL LAST THAT LONG IF WE DO THE JOB WE HAVE TO DO
. . . *rapid redeployment has so depleted american occupation forces here
that it will soon be necessary to use germans to guard military installations a senior officer in the military government said today . . . thirty-
eight year old general gavin who was individually honored today with the
highest order the netherlands can confer may be reduced to his permanent
rank of captain. . . .*

. . . *he said that correspondents might be in a better position than he
was to judge how long public opinion in the unitedstates was likely to
permit american soldiers to stay in europe . . . present plans call for the
reduction of military government personnel in the american zone of
germany to between* 1100 *and* 1200 *officers and civilians . . . thrifty
american soldiers in berlin about* 25000 *of them sent home* $7740203
*last month more than three times as much as they were paid in that
period . . . in explaining why military government functions on the
lower levels are being turned over to the germans clay said we are pulling
out of a job that can best be left to the germans . . .*

. . . *many soldiers when asked to explain where they got their extra
money said it represented gambling winnings it has been said berlin is a
very lucky town where everyone who gambles ends up a winner . . .*
REDEPLOYMENT IMPERILS RULE IN AMERICAN ZONE . . . *my last
trained enlistedman left here last week he said out of* 138 *officers only
sixteen have offered to stay on . . .*

. . . *they get letters from home that tear their hearts out he declared
american women were good soldiers during the war they didn't burden
their husbands with their own troubles and anxieties but now they have
cut loose and are saying what they feel . . . jobs will not be open
indefinitely and they want to go back in time . . . no way of keeping either
officers or enlistedmen who have enough points . . blamed poor planning
for the failure to send qualified civilians here in time . . .* FIRST ARMY
WIVES AND CHILDREN REACH GERMANY TO JOIN TROOPS. . . .

. . . *unitedstates does not intend to turn its back on the problem of
controlling germany . . .*

111

In the evening of January 9, 1946, a crowd of 3,000 G.I.s gathered inside the barbed-wire enclosed compound of General McNarney's headquarters, and stood for forty minutes in the bitter cold chanting "We wanna go home", and listening to speakers who decried the Army leadership from the vantage point of a perch atop a black-out lamp-post. The uniformed men booed and jeered at War Department and Army "brass". When the speeches were over a part of the mob turned and marched on the I.G. Farben building, the Frankfurt pentagon where McNarney had his office. A reinforcement of M.P.s was rushed up, and when the vanguard of the crowd tried to enter the building there was a scuffle, and a score of the demonstrators were detained by the guards. Standing outside the building, the G.I.s announced that they would demonstrate every night until McNarney himself came out to see them.

"Eisenhower came to the front, but McNarney's afraid to come to the front of the building," they shouted derisively. (McNarney was in Berlin at the time.)

It was clear that such rallies bordered on the mutinous. Even in a democracy a soldier is not entitled to imply publicly that his commanding general is a coward. Nothing similar to this could have happened in any other army in the world. It was symptomatic of the deterioration in morale, discipline and organization that had overtaken the Army which only a few months earlier had been the most effective fighting force in the world.

The Army, after yielding to the pressure by the soldiers to accelerate its re-deployment programme, took the then superfluous step of banning any further demonstrations. General McNarney, in issuing the ban, hinted that the rallies might have been promoted or encouraged, or at least exploited, by Communists within the ranks of the soldiers. Voicing the Army's traditional fear and hatred of radicals (which has led it to discriminate against officers who had volunteered to fight Franco in the Spanish Civil War because they were "premature anti-Fascists"), he said:

"A tendency has been noted on some occasions to use the meetings for purposes other than urging more rapid redeployment. . . . Hereafter we must guard against the relatively harmless practice of mass protests for informational purposes from degenerating into an opportunity that may be exploited by some individuals or elements to the extent of becoming definitely injurious to discipline and the good name of the Army."

This rather missed the point. In the first place, the Communists—delicately referred to as "some individuals or elements"—had very little to do with the protests, which would have been held had there not been a single Communist in the Army, and with the same results. In the second place, the demonstrations were "injurious to discipline and the good name of the Army" from their very nature. So was the entire re-deployment programme.

One may call to witness no less an authority than Brigadier General George S. Eyster, who was in charge of re-deployment from the European Theatre. General Eyster wrote in an official report that the point system, on which re-deployment was based, had the following results:—

(1) It "swiftly destroyed the combat efficiency of the U.S. Armed Forces in this theatre".

(2) It "caused to be shipped to the Pacific Ocean area and to the United States units generally incapable of satisfactorily performing their unit missions unless subjected to a minimum of three months training prior to further entry into combat".

(These units would have had to take part in the invasion of Japan except for the intervention of the atom bomb.)

(3) It "was the single greatest cause for the breakdown of discipline which followed V-J Day".

(4) It "rendered ineffective the administrative control on which discipline is based and turned the armies into vast replacement centers".

There were 3,100,000 American soldiers in the European Theatre on May 12, 1945, when re-deployment started. By the end of the year, when the protest meetings were held, 2,500,000 had been shipped out. Units were classified as those which would remain in Germany for the occupation, those which would be shipped to the Pacific area, those which would stay in Europe and be re-trained for a new kind of task before being sent to the Pacific, and those which would be sent home to be demobilized. Men with the highest number of points—

meaning those who had been in service longest and seen the most combat—were put in the last category.

A certain division was slated to return to the States to be de-activated. All of its low-point men—recent replacements—would be taken out of this division, and their place would be filled by high-point men from another division or divisions that were scheduled for occupation or service in the Pacific. The interests of speed and justice were served by this system, the interests of efficiency and discipline were not. By shipping whole divisions at once, the Army was able to evacuate as many as 400,000 men from the theatre in a month. The point system was on the whole fair to the men who had served longest and fought hardest; it was inevitable under any system that G.I.s would gripe at what they considered the slowness of the programme and at individual injustices.

Pfc. Joe Doakes could not understand why there were thirty-six separate stages of re-deployment and why it took him from twenty-five to fifty days from the time he was alerted in Oberpfaffenhofen to the time he walked up the gang-plank of his troopship at Le Havre. During the Battle of the Bulge the entire 82nd Airborne Division had been rushed in twenty-four hours from its rest centre at Reims into contact with the enemy near Houffalize, in the Ardennes, several hundred miles away. There were many other examples of almost equally rapid movements under the pressure of combat necessity. It did not seem logical to the G.I.s that it should take so much longer for their divisions to make routine moves after the fighting was over.

The most disastrous consequences of the point system, how-ever, were the effects on units being kept for the occupation or sent to the Pacific. A division might lose, say, 30 per cent of its personnel, who would be replaced by men from other divisions. Companies and battalions and regiments were broken up, and that most valuable element in morale and discipline, the pride of a soldier in his "outfit", was sacrificed.

"They've taken me away from my buddies", was a common gripe. A soldier's "buddies" were the men who had fought beside him and lived with him in the fox-holes and been ready to risk their lives for his. Moreover the 30 per cent who were taken out were the veteran riflemen, the experienced sergeants and corporals who really hold an army together, and, just as important, the headquarters staffs from company to division,

114

the experts in supply, transportation, engineering, medical services and so on.

Critical officers who saw and understood what was going on wondered frankly what would happen when the reshuffled divisions went into action in the Pacific. One such officer told me later: "I'd hate to think what would have happened if they hadn't dropped that little atom bomb, and we'd had to go in on the beaches of Japan".

It can only be guessed how many lives would have been needlessly lost; but the effects on the Army of Occupation in Germany need not be the subject for conjecture. The main concern of the men, and not only of men, but of officers, was to watch their points, try to figure out when they would get home, and in the meantime concentrate their efforts on securing frauleins, liquor and loot. Point consciousness was greatly stimulated by the *Stars and Stripes*, the soldier newspaper which showed great ingenuity but little sense of responsibility in the way it managed to produce daily stories, printed under banner headlines, giving the latest news, or, if there was none, "making" news about the progress or lack of progress of re-deployment.

Little was done by the Army to explain to the soldiers their responsibilities as Americans in Europe, to make them understand the need for discipline, or even to suggest that they might take advantage of the unique educational opportunity given them by their free trip to Europe. "They can have this country", was a frequently heard remark, and it was applied not only to Germany, but to France and Belgium and England as well. Dozens of times I heard officers and enlisted men declare solemnly: "Give me the worst dump in America ahead of any place I've seen in Europe."

To America's allies and to the vanquished Germans the spectacle of the disintegration of our Army was amazing and unpleasantly revealing. My arguments with Frenchmen about German policy usually ended up with my interlocutor shrugging his shoulders and remarking: "Mais vous ne resterez pas en Allemagne: c'est une autre affaire pour nous qui devons vivre à côté des boches." ("But you won't be staying in Germany; it's quite a different matter for us who have to go on living next to the krauts.")

Dozens of Germans have asked me apprehensively: "How much longer will the Americans stay in Berlin? Aren't the

Russians going to take over soon?" They considered us the lesser evil, but down in the zone, where we were the sole occupiers, many of them regarded our expected imminent departure with greater equanimity.

The dramatic melting away of our Army made the voices of our statesmen ring hollow at the conference tables. The American people, instead of asking peevishly and unthinkingly "Why don't we have a policy in Germany?" would have done far better to have asked how any policy could be carried out effectively when they themselves were clamouring for the destruction of the instrument which should have backed up that policy. Until the world devises a better system, diplomacy will continue to be based on military strength. This may be an unpleasant fact, but it is a fact none the less. It is far better to talk softly but let everyone know that there is something substantial behind the words than to use tough language and have nothing behind it, as has too often been the American practice.

Still more unfortunate than our actual military weakness (air force officers say that there was a time when we could not have put one squadron of bombers into the air) were the implications to the average European of our actions. When every American was crying "I wanna go home", the European assumed that soon he would go home. The French felt they could not afford to base their policy on the assumption that the United States would continue to take an active interest in Europe. The Germans could not take our occupation too seriously when everything they saw suggested that it could not last long. I have suggested that I believed Clay was right in turning the responsibility for many local matters back to the Germans more quickly than many of his critics believed was wise. But he should have been able to do it because he thought it was right, and not have to let it be suspected that he did it because he had no alternative. He was forced to lead from weakness instead of from strength.

The same thing applies to Byrnes' proposal for a twenty-five-year treaty with Russia, Britain and France to keep Germany from re-arming. Byrnes said the treaty would permit an early end to mass occupation of Germany. He hoped the fact that he was proposing it would convince America's allies that America did not mean to withdraw from European affairs. But many Englishmen and Frenchmen told me they were convinced

116

Byrnes proposed an early end of the occupation, not because he thought it was wise, but because he knew the American public was unwilling to keep an army in Europe. They could not help wondering whether a treaty designed to go into effect only after the end of the occupation was proposed so early because Mr. Byrnes was afraid that at some later date the American Senate would fail to approve such a treaty.

The American public acted unrealistically and inconsistently. It demanded that its government be rough on the Germans, tough with the Russians—and bring the boys home. These aims were patently incompatible. And not only did Americans want to bring back the boys who had fought in the war, but they were reluctant to send over anyone to take their places. It was uncertainty about the continued flow of draftees and volunteers into the Army that caused the Army to slow down its planned schedule for re-deployment for the first half of 1946. This in turn caused the mass protests by the soldiers. They saw their departure dates being postponed, and wanted definite new dates fixed. General Eisenhower was forced to agree to a dangerously accelerated re-deployment schedule.

By the beginning of 1946 morale and discipline in the occupation Army had reached their lowest ebb. One G.I., Pfc. John I. Shields, the editor of a soldier newspaper in Lugwigsburg near Stuttgart, wrote at that time:

"The average soldier in Germany learns only two things from his occupational experience. He learns how to drink and how to pick up a fraulein. His assigned job is taken for granted because in most cases it requires only physical presence. His attitudes, outside of wanting to go home, are mainly gripes about the Army caste system and 'why doesn't somebody else get on the ball?'

"From a military point of view, our duty here is to destroy completely the German's ability to make war and to wipe out the Nazi and militaristic influence implanted in the German mind. But thinking of ourselves, as individual citizens of a peace-loving world, our mission is extended beyond this. Our mission here is to foster the re-education of the German people through limited but personal contacts with them.

"We ourselves are not prone to believe the over-all statements of higher authorities, articles suspected of incorporating propaganda, or opinions offered without justifying reasons. We have to see to believe. We know that the Army is chicken, no matter what the re-enlistment posters say.

"The German people are like this, too. They must see to believe. They must see the fallacies of their former ways of life before they will be in a position to accept the programs which we bring to them. They must realize the individual influence that each exerted in permitting a war before they can accept the individual responsibility of helping to prevent another one.

"The success of our civilian mission here does not depend upon the policies set by the big boys in Washington or by the boys whose shoulders are stooped with brass. It depends upon the lowly G.I., who is frowned upon and spit upon by the Army caste system but who, nevertheless, holds the key to the success of this mission on his fingertips.

"It is by establishing friendships of a constructive and enlightening nature, by presenting the habits of conduct to which we are accustomed at home and by being cautious of misplaced sympathy that this goal can best be reached."

It is deplorable that there were not more people in the Army, and people of rank higher than private first class, with the sense and courage to speak out to the soldiers this way. The Army caste system of which he spoke is something very real. In the front lines there was genuine friendship and camaraderie between officers and men. When the fighting was over, however, the soldier came back to rest areas, where he found red tape and discrimination. He found towns posted off limits. In other towns the best hotels and restaurants would be labelled "Off Limits to Enlisted Personnel". Exaggerated saluting was enforced—and resented by the soldier, who found too many officers unworthy of the respect implied in the salute.

This discrimination was extended to U.S. civilians employed by or attached to the Army. In some places they were excluded from officers' messes. They had to pay for their billets, while officers of equivalent rank got theirs—better ones—free. This discrimination included such trivial but annoying phenomena as the issuance of inferior liquor rations to civilians. When dependents were brought to Europe, Army officers' wives were given preferential treatment.

The United States Army is probably on the whole more democratic than any other, but an army just isn't a democratic institution. The soldier-citizens of a democracy resented this. For the most part they were not anxious to re-enlist, though many may have changed their minds upon getting home to find that the country they were returning to as men was not quite as they had remembered leaving it as boys.

It became apparent to the Army chiefs that their soldiers, whom Eisenhower had called "ambassadors of democracy", were failing in their mission. They had reason to speculate about how long the German population would remain docile if the occupying Army continued to show neither physical nor moral strength. It was of this thought that was born the Constabulary—the mobile security force that would be the occupation when the infantry divisions had gone home.

The Constabulary was conceived of necessity—the necessity created by re-deployment and the breakdown of discipline and morale. The existing units had lost their *esprit de corps*: a new unit should be formed and imbued with a new *esprit de corps*. There were not enough troops left to garrison even fairly large towns, while the countryside might rarely see an occupation soldier: the new mobile force would have to move about constantly as an evidence to the Germans of the presence of the Americans.

The men in this force had to have discipline, pride in their outfit, a consciousness of their mission and its importance. The name "constabulary" gave a romantic touch designed to stimulate that pride. It was taken from the Philippine Constabulary of an earlier occupation. It conveyed the suggestion of a dashing, mounted police force. It was just that—except that the men were mounted on tanks, half-tracks, armoured cars, motor-cycles and jeeps instead of on thoroughbred chargers. As these vehicles rumbled and sped through the zone, the Germans were, presumably, impressed. This in turn served to impress the G.Is. with themselves—an important point, since the rehabilitation of the G.I. was the first purpose of the Army in forming the Constabulary.

The trooper was dressed up in a flashy uniform—blue-and-gold-striped helmet liner, Sam Browne belt, golden neckerchief of parachute silk and paratrooper boots. He carried either a Colt automatic, a carbine or a tommy gun. On his shoulder was the conspicuous patch of the Constabulary—a blue "C" on a golden-yellow background with superimposed red thunderbolt.

All this was to give the Constabulary "colour". The force also got a colourful commander, Major General Ernest N. Harmon, a typical World War II tank commander. Typical, I should say, of the best tank commanders. For he had led the 1st and 2nd Armoured Divisions from Kasserine Pass and Sicily over the Normandy beaches, through the Ardennes and across Germany to the Elbe.

James O'Donnell, writing in *Newsweek* (August 26, 1946), compared Harmon with Patton—and not to Harmon's disadvantage. O'Donnell wrote:

"An Army formation is never better than its commanding officer, and just as there was a little bit of Patton in every Third Army soldier, so is there a touch of Harmon in the troopers. Harmon, like Ethan Allen one of the most untypical of Vermonters, is a fighting general in the best 'Hell on Wheels' tradition. He is a mustached and more jovial Patton. Patton was shrill. Harmon roars like a bull. To the charge that he is making the Constabulary a glorified cavalry, Harmon growls good-naturedly: 'And what in hell's the matter with the cavalry?'

"Like Patton, Harmon has a thunderous command of all the blunt words from the Anglo-Saxon base of the language, and uses them when the occasion warrants. Like Patton he has color and showmanship, just the proper touch of fustian and bombast. When his streamlined train roars into Munich, he is met by an honor guard standing at rigid attention. The cavalcade speeds across the city with wailing sirens and along roped-off thoroughfares. Behind snappy trooper cordons crowd the Muencheners, who refer to this performance as 'The Second Coming'. Nothing irreligious—just that Patton was once here.

"At home, Harmon's emphasis on sharp saluting, iron discipline, and correct wearing of the uniform might be dismissed as spit-and-polish garrison soldiering. In Germany, it is the *sine qua non* of successful occupation. Harmon says: 'Dammit, twice in 25 years these —— krauts all but conquered the —— world. You can't pretend to be a soldier before such a critical audience. You've got to be one. And the first step toward being one is to look like one.' "

The Constabulary looked like a good solution to the occupation force's re-deployment problem. Although its personnel requirements were numerically much more modest, military government was stricken just as badly by re-deployment as the Army proper. Military government did not need many men, but it needed qualified men, and those with experience and ability were all going home. Officers who had volunteered for the job of military government and had been given specific training for the job on the understanding that they would stay with it for several years after the end of hostilities rushed back under the point system. When the war ended, their job was just beginning, but they had no further interest in it. They had to be replaced by men without training or experience.

Top men in the Army recognized that in the long run military government would be best run not by the military but by civilians. Over 50 per cent of the military personnel in military government were to be replaced with civilians by June 1, 1946. Unfortunately the trained civilians did not exist in sufficient numbers, and were not sent over as fast as the Army men were discharged. Our occupation was terribly handicapped during the first year by the lack of personnel, by the lack of interest on the part of those who were in Germany but knew they would be leaving soon, and by the constant reshuffling that went on. Military government officers would be replaced again and again, making for lack of continuity. The Germans were bewildered by having to deal with men unfamiliar with the local situation, men who did not know what had happened under their predecessors and who would themselves be replaced as soon as they had mastered their job.

The man who did volunteer to stay on, very likely taking back his old job as a civilian at a higher salary, was generally among the least competent: he was the man who feared he could not get as good a job at home, or the man who wanted to stay because he could live cheaply and make money on the black market. It would be unfair not to add that there was a minority of high-minded men who felt they had a job to do and idealistically shouldered their responsibility.

In Berlin, Colonel Frank L. Howley managed to hold together a military government team that was a credit to the United States and compared favourably with those of other nations in a city where comparisons were inevitably made. Unfortunately, Howley and his team were an exception.

Many officers and soldiers began to show up again in Germany as civilians a few months after they had gone home, having found that the high cost of living, the paucity of good jobs, or the difficulty of readjusting to a pedestrian life after the excitement and stimulation of several years overseas made the United States less of a paradise than they had dreamily imagined in the "We wanna go home" period. But these, too, were rarely the highest calibre men.

There is no easy answer. The worst of re-deployment chaos is over. There remains the need for a permanent army large enough to permit the United States to fulfil its international commitments. Behind this lies the need for Americans to develop an intelligent interest in foreign affairs and an awareness that what goes on beyond the oceans will continue to affect the lives of individual Americans whether they are interested in it or not. The Germans have sinned by commission. The Americans have sinned by omission, and show a tendency to continue doing so. Americans as well as Germans need to be educated to the responsibilities of democracy—and they have nobody but themselves to help them.

VIII

TWO GERMANIES, TWO EUROPES, TWO WORLDS

News Picture

. . . the ability of the big three to agree on a policy for treating germany as an economic whole has been regarded generally as the criterion by which the success . . . ZUKOV SETS UP GERMAN REGIME IN SOVIET ZONE . . . *historic change is being wrought without any directives or even explicit approval from the allied control council which nominally rules germany . . .* REDS MAY TAKE GERMAN OUTPUT AS REPARATIONS . . . FRANCE BLOCKS POTSDAM PLAN FOR GERMANY . . . *french are determined that the rhineland and the industrial ruhr valley in westphalia shall be detached from the rest of germany . . .*

. . if it should prove impossible to break down the economic barriers constituted by the present zonal boundaries . . . ONE GERMANY OR FOUR IS ISSUE AT PARIS PARLEY . . . BERLIN PAPERS FEATURE LACK OF BIG 4 ACCORD. . . .

. . . AMERICAN ZONE ISSUES BAN ON PLANT REMOVALS REPARATIONS HALTED UNTIL POWERS TREAT GERMANY AS AN ECONOMIC WHOLE . . . MOLOTOV HITS BYRNES PLAN FOR GERMANY . . . *went on to charge that the unitedstates britain and france are not living up to the potsdam agreement and said the suspension of reparations shipments of machinery from the american occupation zone of germany to the soviet union is unlawful . . . evident that the american and russian views on germany are still far apart . . . molotov was particularly concerned about reparations . . .*

BYRNES OFFERS NEW PROPOSAL ON GERMANY

US WILL JOIN WITH ANY OTHER POWER TO UNITE THE ZONE ECONOMICALLY

DENIES HE SEEKS VENGEANCE PEACE

TELLS BIG 4 HE PREFERS GERMANY TO BE TREATED AS AN ECONOMIC WHOLE

BIG 4 ADJOURN FAIL TO AGREE ON GERMANY

. . . unitedstates and britain will go ahead with plans to form their own occupation zone into a single economic unit . . .

GENERAL PIERRE JOSEPH KOENIG, the tall Frenchman who is honoured by his fellow-countrymen as the "hero of Bir Hacheim", laid down his cylindrical hat, his gloves and his swagger stick, and took the chair at the meeting of the Allied Control Council. The Americans, Russians and British facing and flanking him on the other three sides of the square of tables in the large conference room waited for him to open the meeting and then listened carefully to his exposition, spoken in precise French.

It was one of the Control Council's first meetings, Koenig was explaining France's objections to the central German administrations which the other three delegations were trying to establish in accordance with the Potsdam decisions.

The words flowed on: French Government, which is not a party to the Potsdam Agreement, requested its Allies to exchange views . . . before it could associate itself with the responsibilities. . . .

Koenig paused and sat smiling as though he had been giving a pleasant, inconsequential after-dinner talk, while the two interpreters standing behind his chair gave expressionless renditions of his words in Russian and English.

. . . establishment of central German administrations was one of those points which made necessary the most important French reservations . . . French Member of the Allied Control Council in Berlin will not be authorized to agree to any measure prejudicing the future of the Rheno-Westphalian region until the question has been discussed and agreed upon by the ministers . . . but whatever may be the limits assigned to the functions of the proposed central administrations, the very principle of their establishment prejudges the status of the regions concerned . . . obliged in accordance with the instructions of my Government to ask that the study of the two proposals on the establishment of central administrations which are submitted for consideration by the Control Council be postponed. At present I could not but reject these proposals . . .

The Council decided to postpone study of the papers. The postponement proved to be an indefinite one. Every month the regular American report on military government in Germany stated laconically: "The French delegation maintained its objections to the establishment of the Potsdam central administrative agencies for Germany", or words to that effect.

I have explained how the exclusion of France from Potsdam led to the anomalous situation where one of the four occupation Powers had not agreed to the principles upon which the other three proposed to base that occupation, yet was given the power to veto any action.

The French also vetoed national trades unions and national political parties, as well as central administrations. They saw through and opposed every plan to achieve even the mildest kind of administrative centralization. They even refused to agree to uniform postage stamps for Germany. When General de Gaulle, at that time still the President of the French Provisional Government, was asked for his views, he stated bluntly: "We do not want any more Reich." With logical, stubborn consistency, the French stuck to their position and would not budge or compromise.

General Clay saw in the proposed central agencies the first step towards the economic unification of Germany. These departments would not have constituted a German Government in any sense; they corresponded to the technical ministries in a Cabinet. Transportation, communications, finance, foreign trade and industry must be centrally administered in a modern State, even a relatively decentralized one. To these five Clay proposed adding a department of food and agriculture. The four Powers would have to get together to select the German personnel of the agencies. These Germans would be given the right of free circulation for themselves and their representatives throughout the four zones. They would be responsible to the Control Council in Berlin. Local military authorities would not have the right to interfere with or give orders to German personnel of the agencies operating in the zones.

It is doubtful whether the Russians would have been willing to grant so much freedom to central German agencies operating in their zone. The French veto made it impossible for the Council to ascertain this. The Russians could say with justice that the French were blocking the economic unity of Germany. They went further than this: they suggested that if the Americans and British were sincerely in favour of economic unity they would find ways to force the French to accept the principle. One American official of the Allied Control Authority told me: "I tried to explain to the Russians that we don't use such methods in our diplomacy but he was sure we would use them to get something we wanted badly enough." Then he added with a smile: "And of course we do!"

The French were using the central agencies as a bargaining point to get what they wanted in western Germany. They argued, with some justice, that the eastern boundaries of Germany had been fixed, if not formally, at least practically, in such a way that it would be difficult to revise them. Why, then, should not the western frontiers be fixed in the same way? The industries of the Ruhr had constituted the main productive potential for Germany in two wars: therefore the area should be detached from Germany and internationalized. The Rhine bridgeheads had been the springboard for two German attacks on France: therefore the Rhineland should be detached from the rest of Germany and should become an independent State.

A unified Germany that included the Ruhr and Rhineland would be strong enough to menace France within another generation, the French argued. They apparently had little faith in the effectiveness of plans for military and industrial disarmament of Germany. They regarded any proposals for an international economic control commission for the Ruhr as insufficient without political control. They expressed their fears that the United States, for instance, would not remain long in Germany to enforce such controls. They also knew from their own experience under the German occupation how controls can be circumvented.

In reality the French feared a unified Germany because of the possibility that it would be dominated by the Russians from Berlin at least as much as because of the likelihood of the resurgence of Germany itself as a potential aggressor. They wished to detach the strategically and economically vital areas of western Germany so that if Russia gained control of the rest of Germany it would not have gained anything decisive. The trend of thought of De Gaulle and Bidault was that Westphalia and the Rhineland could be incorporated into a Western bloc that would be a counter to the Eastern bloc the Russians seemed to be forming. Viewed in this light, Russian opposition to the French proposals and Russian suspicions of Britain and the United States for not putting more pressure on France to accept the central administrations are easy to understand.

Maurice Thorez and his French Communists backed Bidault's party in demanding vociferously that the Ruhr and Rhineland be taken from Germany. It was the popular thing to do in France, and the Communists wanted votes. In Germany it was just as popular to favour retention of these areas; and that is what the German Communists did. They were backed up by Molotov, who thereby put the French comrades on the spot.

If Germany was not to be treated as an economic unit, it was clear that eventually it would split down the middle, first economically and then politically. Eastern Germany would have to turn round economically and find in eastern Europe the resources and markets it normally had in western Germany. Similarly, western Germany would have to face around to the west. The complicated interdependence of the various parts of Germany, having broken down, would have to be replaced with something else. This would mean a big readjustment involving initial hardship and great economic inefficiency, but it was a possible solution. It was certainly not the solution envisaged at Potsdam. It would mean drawing a sharp line through the middle of Germany, and of Europe. This line would be a frontier separating the "two worlds", and replacing the present amorphous border area.

The Russians, unwilling to accept such a development as inevitable, were nevertheless taking steps to organize the parts of Europe they controlled in such a way that they would be prepared for it if it came. The steps they took, such as economic centralization of their German zone, tended to make this development more likely. The Americans wanted to wait as long as possible before doing anything that might prejudice the one Germany, one Europe, one world solution.

One of the chief reasons for American impatience with the French attitude was that it beclouded the issues in Germany. If the Russians were not prepared to carry out the economic unity provisions of Potsdam, the sooner one found that out the better. The French veto provided the Russians with a beautiful "out" if they wished to shelve the inconvenient provisions of Potsdam without putting themselves technically in the wrong.

There were other things besides the formation of central agencies that needed to be done if Germany was to become an economic unit. It was necessary to use the resources of all the German zones for the benefit of Germany as a whole. It was necessary to use all exports to pay for needed imports, even if that meant paying for imports into one zone with exports from

127

another. The American zone was particularly dependent on the other zones. A large part of its modest industry was engaged in assembling products from other zones. It lacked coal. It has been said: "The Russians got the wheat in Germany, the British got the coal and the Americans got the mountains."

There is a truth in this obvious over-simplification. Clay once listened to a correspondent who had just returned from a visit to the Soviet zone and was telling how much greater progress had been made there in reviving industrial production than in the American zone. Clay remarked dryly: "It's not my fault if I was given the only zone without any coal."

On another occasion he told his Russian, French and British colleagues on the Co-ordinating Committee: "The areas allocated to the United States are rich in scenic beauty but were accepted only on the understanding that the resources of all Germany were to be available for the support of Germany as a whole."

Once agreement had been reached on the future level of the German economy, all excess plant capacity having been declared available for reparations (March, 1946), the Americans and British began to press for the adoption of an export–import plan. The level of industry agreement was based on the assumption that Germany would be treated as an economic whole; and common policies on foreign trade were essential to such treatment.

The Economics Directorate, after studying the problem of exports and imports, came up with a majority and a minority report. The latter, giving the views of the Soviet member, stated: "For the immediate future foreign trade for Germany should be conducted on a zonal basis within the net balance of each zone. Barter transactions should be permitted and the payment for allowed exports may be made by allowed imports."

This barter system involved trade agreements between the zones, and was more cumbersome than the normal procedures in the trade between sovereign nations. The Russians were willing to make such agreements in order to get commodities they needed from the other zones. They were not willing to permit free trade throughout Germany lest their zone make a disproportionate contribution to the general economy. Nor did they wish the other Powers to exercise any form of control over, or even get reliable information about, "exports" from the Soviet zone, which were mainly in the form of products manufactured by processing raw materials imported from the east.

Most of the stocks and current production that went to the Soviet Union from the Russian zone were not classed as exports at all, but as "reparations". The Russians kept no accounting of these reparations, or, if they did, they did not inform their allies. The Western Allies had never agreed in principle that reparations should come from current production: before doing so they would certainly have insisted that the level of industry be revised upward, that a figure for the total of reparations be fixed and announced, and that facilities be granted for checking the amounts of such reparations being taken.

The majority reports, giving the views of the British, French and American members of the Economics directorate, stated:

"Common policies should now be established, including appropriate settlement of the present deficit in regard to import and export programmes for Germany as a whole; this requires:—

(1) equitable distribution of indigenous resources,
(2) uniform standards for the approval of imports,
(3) sharing of responsibility for financing imports,
(4) sharing of proceeds from exports,
(5) observance of the principle that the proceeds of exports from current production and stocks shall be available in the first place for payment of approved imports,
(6) uniform policies with respect to prices and currencies received in payment for exports,
(7) uniform provisions for accounting, auditing and maintenance of statistical data regarding imports and exports."

The British suggested further that "any deficit shown at the end of a given period should be made good by the occupying powers in proportion to the population of the zones, in the form of a loan to the import-export account, to be made good out of any surpluses which may ultimately be shown, ranking

E   (Struggle for Germany)   129 before any contribution to costs of occupation". The United States could not agree to this arrangement because the use of American appropriations is limited by law to specific items.

The showdown on exports and imports came in the Co-ordinating Committee one month to the day (April 26) after the level of industry plan was signed. General Koeltz said the French delegation could not accept any method which did not treat Germany as an economic entity, which was also a principle of the Potsdam Agreement. He said that pooling of economic resources was essential, and that the French zone in particular was a poor one and needed assistance from the other zones. This statement was pounced upon with some glee by the Soviet member, General Dratvin, who asked whether the French position with regard to central agencies had changed, in view of General Koeltz's reference to the principle of German economic unity as contained in the Potsdam Agreement.

Koeltz said there was no need of such agencies for the purpose of treating Germany as an economic unit. Clay asked whether the Soviet position on exports and imports resulted from the present lack of central administrative machinery. Dratvin replied that the question he had directed to General Koeltz had the purpose of clarifying the entire situation, and that since Koeltz's answer confirmed the original French position on this matter, he fully supported the position of his delegates in the Economics Directorate.

Clay then suggested referring to the Governments the entire question of reparations, import and export policy and central machinery as interdependent questions requiring integrated decision at the governmental level. Dratvin argued that once equipment available for reparations had been determined, there was no connection between reparations and exports and imports. Clay pointed out that none of the main economic provisions of the Potsdam Declaration had been executed within nearly a year of occupation, and said he must report to his Government that the point had been reached when there must be a decision as to whether Potsdam would be carried out as a whole or not.

Koeltz recalled that the French Government had requested consideration by its Allies of the whole German problem for many months. In February the French Government had specifically requested that the question of central German

130

organizations be studied. He believed there were other ways than central administrations for implementing the export–import policy.

At this *impasse* Clay played his ace of trumps, announcing that in view of the close connection between the export–import programme and the reparations programme, the United States Delegation must now definitely stop the work of between 16,000 and 17,000 men who were dismantling factories for delivery as reparations. This ended the discussion.

It also turned the level of industry agreement into an interesting historical document just one month after it had been signed. The Russians wanted to take the reparations to which this agreement entitled them and then talk about treating Germany as an economic whole. Clay thought this was putting the cart before the horse. He wanted to make sure the American zone could rely on the resources of the rest of Germany before he stripped down its industrial capacity.

If he had not done this, the Americans might one day have found themselves in the position of being financially responsible for a zone which had given away half of its already modest plant capacity and could not hope, in such circumstances, to be self-supporting. It would have been a permanent drain on the United States Treasury. Once the reparations plants had been removed and delivered, the United States would also have lost its bargaining power.

The next logical step was Byrnes' offer to amalgamate the American zone economically with any or all others. It seemed likely that the offer would not be accepted by any but the British. In that case the result would be a strengthening of the trend towards splitting Germany down the middle. However, the Americans felt they must do whatever they could to relieve the critical economic situation in Germany and reduce the financial burden of the occupation zone on the American tax-payer. By making the union offer to all three of the other nations, and by keeping it open, the United States would avoid the onus of splitting Germany if that should eventually happen.

At the same time an attempt was made to compose America's differences with France. It was hoped that the French, in exchange for the Saar, would agree to leave the Ruhr and Rhineland in Germany with suitable controls over their heavy industry, and would withdraw their objections to central administrations.

131

IX

WE AND THE RUSSIANS

News Picture

. . . marshal koniev a bald stocky man with quiet friendly eyes welcomed the american general on the steps of the large house which is surrounded by spacious lawns and took him up to the most lavish of all the banquets the russians have produced for the americans in the last ten days . . .

10,000 A DAY RUSSIANS CROSS ELBE TO SOVIET LINES AND HOME SCENE AT MAGDEBURG DESCRIBED

WEARY RANKS OF UPROOTED HUMANITY THREEFOURTHS OF THEM WOMEN MARCH OVER BRIDGE TO RED WELCOME

. . . berlin still is being run in the russian way . . . in all my dealings with the russians i have found them completely ready to help wherever we have needed help i cannot believe there is any problem facing us which cannot be solved. . . .

POLAND FACING VAST PROBLEMS IN POMERANIA

STACKED GRAIN ROTS IN FIELD AS POLES RESPOND SLOWLY TO
   APPEALS TO SETTLE LAND

. . . a polish official here told the following story the polish district chiefs of this province met with a russian colonel at koszalin to discuss administration problems they complained to him that soviet removals were stripping the country and making their work impossible the russian colonel replied in the fourteenth century this was a polish land ruled by king boleslaw the wrymouthed at that time these machines and these cows were not here we are returning the land to you just as it was when boleslaw lost it 600 years ago. . . .

. . . THOUSANDS FLEE GERMAN AREA CEDED TO POLAND *. . .*
ZHUKOV SETS UP GERMAN REGIME IN SOVIET ZONE *. . . move to split up the estates and turn them over to the peasants is being led by the communists . . . free german trades union association the communists thus obtained half of the places on the central committee. . . .*

. . . ZHUKOV WITHDRAWS RED TEAM
   GIS WIN BERLIN TRACK MEET

. . . RUSSIANS STILL IN FULL CONTROL OF BERLIN RADIO *. . . studios are in the british sector the transmitter is in the french sector the lines run through the american sector and the station is operated by the russians that is fourpower cooperation . . .*

132

... REDS MAY TAKE GERMAN OUTPUT AS REPARATIONS ...
PATTON REMOVAL PRAISED IN RED ZONE OF BERLIN ... INDEX OF
BANNED BOOKS PREPARED FOR BERLIN ... GERMAN REDS AND
SOCIALISTS STUDY MERGER ... *redarmy newspaper taegliche rundschau
attacked the americanlicensed tagesspiegel*. ...
... RUSSIANS GRANT ... RUSSIA MOVES ... RUSSIANS BAN ...
*became apparent that there was more method in the russians action than
many of the germans had believed.* ...
GERMANS SPUR PRODUCTION IN RUSSIAN ZONE ... *president is a
socialdemocrat the first vicepresident is a communist.* ...
REDS IN BERLIN HEAR ATTACK ON POLICY OF ALLIES ...
US ARMY BARS ATTACK ON ALLIES BY BERLIN REDS. ...
FURTWAENGLER FLIES TO BERLIN RED ZONE
US BARRED CONDUCTOR IS BROUGHT IN BY RUSSIANS
... US SENTENCES 2 BERLIN REDS TO 5 YEARS EACH ... SOCIALIST
RED UNITY PARTY IS SET UP IN BERLIN ... REDS AT BORDER TAKE
GERMANS OFF US TRAINS ... RUSSIANS ORDER RADIO STATION FOR
BERLIN ZONE ... REDS SOCIALISTS ... RUSSIANS TAKE MORE
MACHINES FROM RED ZONE ... BERLIN THRONGS MARK MAY DAY
... *if molotov is seriously interested in having this investigation made
byrnes said all he has to do is to pick up the telephone and give instruc-
tions to his representative in berlin and the matter will be arranged.* ...
RUSSIA BACKS UNIFICATION OF GERMANY STRESSES ITS ROLE IN
WORLD ECONOMY MOLOTOV HITS HARD PEACE OPPOSES AGRARIAN
PLAN OR SEPARATION OF RUHR HE REBUFFS FRANCE AFTER
BIDAULT PLEA WOULD ALLOW MORE STEEL OUTPUT WITH SAFE-
GUARD SHIFT IN KREMLIN SEEN

THE American Army's first meeting with the Russians was
symbolical of subsequent relations. The 9th and 1st
Armies had been dashing across northern Germany, with the
British 2nd Army on their left flank and the American
3rd Army on their right. The 9th Army had crossed the
Elbe north of Magdeburg and was building up in its bridgehead for a drive on Berlin. Suddenly a cryptic order to halt was
received. The 9th Army had to draw back behind the Elbe;
the 1st Army was not to proceed beyond the Mulde. For
about a week the armies waited, sent patrols up to five miles
beyond the rivers, met no German fighting formations and no
Russians. There was nothing but a wandering mass of freed
"slave labourers", German civilians anxious to cross into

American-held territory and disorganized Wehrmacht soldiers trying to surrender.

The whole thing seemed mysterious to the American troops: the unexplained order to stop advancing; the reports, never substantiated, of Russian columns sighted; the broadcasts over Russian field radios telling the Americans to stay where they were, that they (the Russians) were advancing as fast as they could and would meet them the next day (which they didn't, although there was nothing to stop them from advancing). The official explanation, given later, cleared up some of the mystery: if the two armies had kept advancing towards each other there would very likely have been mistakes, incidents, disputes. It was better to draw up on natural lines and let patrols make the contact. It was not added, though it was true, that the Russians wanted the prestige of capturing Berlin single-handed (although it would have cost them fewer lives to have done it with American help); and that they wanted to be the sole occupiers of Berlin during the important initial period, so that they could organize the civil administration and could remove "reparations" machinery from the western part of the city.

The actual first meeting with the Russians occurred because an American divisional commander disobeyed orders and let a patrol go twenty-five miles beyond the Mulde to the Elbe. The Russians were on the far side, and came across to shake hands and have their pictures taken.

G.I.s and G. Ivans got along pretty well together at first. They fraternized as much as they could, considering that they had no common language. They traded watches (until the Americans realized that behind this touching Russian desire to exchange souvenirs lay a clear awareness that American watches were better). They found that in many ways the American and Russian characters were akin: particularly in their love of the big, the young and the new, in an outlook on life that comes from living in a country where there are great spaces, a country that is doing things on a big scale. They had mutual respect, too, for the power of each other's armies and military achievements.

The generals also got along well together, as long as they were inviting each other to banquets and toasting the imminent defeat of Nazi Germany and the magnificent victories of the great Red Army which had come from Stalingrad and the great American Army which had come from Normandy, and the great Marshal Stalin and the great President Roosevelt. The Americans were a little taken aback when the Russians, after sitting quietly before an untouched banquet while Marshal Koniev made his speech, dug into the food with a great clatter of plates and forks and commotion of reaching for platters while General Bradley was replying. They did not think it very tactful either that the Russians in all their pretty speeches mentioned their hope that President Truman would follow the policy of his great predecessor (plainly implying that they feared he would not; implying, as well, that they had a right to suggest what American policy should be).

Taken all in all, however, the first contacts with the Russians were friendly. The Americans found the Russians cordial and often helpful. Where they were not helpful, it was usually that they had received some specific order; in such cases their embarrassment at not being able to do what had been requested of them, and not wanting to say so, made them act in a way that seemed rather mysterious to Americans. It is an American trait to like a straightforward answer, and they were baffled by what seemed to them an Oriental coquettishness on the part of the Russians, an inability to say yes and an unwillingness to say no.

In the first year of occupation there must have been thousands of quadripartite meetings on various levels of authority. In these meetings the Americans had a pretty good chance to learn how the Russians operate. One thing they noticed was that the Russians liked these meetings; they enjoyed playing around with the quadripartite machinery, bargaining, invoking technical rules, referring matters from one committee to another. Another thing was that the Russians had less authority to negotiate, make quick decisions or concessions than the Americans or British or even the French (except where central administrations were concerned). It was rare that a Russian of lower rank than General Sokolovsky could make an important decision; and frequently the decision could not be made in Germany at all.

Thus it took a long time before it became quite clear that the Russian hiding behind procedures itself hid basic policy conflicts and a great deal of suspicion. The suspicion, which was mutual, became intensified as the months went on, even though in Berlin, where there was daily contact, relations were much better than in the capitals where the Foreign Ministers met. It was not a personalized suspicion, because the American colonel on, say, the Economics Directorate was quite prepared to believe that his Russian opposite number was an honest, trustworthy individual. The Russian would concede the same about the American.

But the American soon decided that the Russian, because he was a part of the Soviet system, was not in a position to act as an individual. Therefore, no matter how much they enjoyed themselves together over a bottle of vodka or whisky, the Russian was going to veto the proposal the American was going to make at the next morning's meeting, and would probably imply that this proposal was not only unacceptable but basically Fascist-inspired and in violation of the Potsdam Agreement. In turn the Russian was convinced that the American, no matter how good a fellow he seemed to be, was at best an unwitting tool of sinister capitalist interests planning an encirclement of the Soviet Union.

Americans usually laugh at the idea that the Russians may feel themselves threatened or encircled. Yet this has un-doubtedly been a real fear, despite Mr. Stalin's disclaimer. In spite of everything the official propaganda says about how the Red Army won the war practically single-handed and is the mightiest in the world, the Russian leaders have some idea, though certainly not an entirely accurate one, of the strength of the Western Powers. They know the United States is industrially a long way ahead of them. Of course they fear the atom bomb. And with all their knowledge of what we possess, they have not very much faith in our motives.

Americans have no greater faith in theirs. They ask them-selves: "What do the Russians really want?" It looked as though the Russians wanted to spread their influence and control in Germany as far as possible, to dominate the country completely if they could. Whether they wished to do so as a step towards spreading Communism throughout the world, or in order to make the borders of Russia more secure, or because the leaders of the Soviet Union, prisoners of their own power, could not help trying to extend that power, must be left unanswered here. There probably is no single, simple answer. The other occupying Powers were unwilling to accept such an extension of Soviet influence and control: consequently a conflict and struggle for power were inevitable.

The Russians entered this struggle at what might be considered a propitious time for them. The end of the war in Europe seemed likely to create what Lenin would have called a revolutionary situation. Property relations had been disrupted by the Nazis and by the war. In Europe there was general disillusion with capitalism. Socialism seemed to many, perhaps to the majority, to be the answer. When Hitler seized power, Germany, the birthplace of Marxism, had the strongest Communist party in Europe outside Russia. Yet the Russians lost the first round of this struggle, in Germany as in most of the other countries of Europe.

The causes are not hard to find. They lie largely in the colossal blunders and miscalculations and misjudgments made by the Russians themselves. It is true that in Germany they laboured under one big disadvantage—namely, the traditional anti-Slavic feeling of the Germans. This was combined in the middle class with a fear of Communism. The two had been ably exploited by Hitler and Goebbels. Yet these were not insurmountable obstacles. The Russians could very well have proved Goebbels wrong; instead, they made a very good effort at proving him right.

There is no question that the tales the Berliners poured into the ears of the Americans about rape and loot and indiscriminate removals were exaggerated. But there is no doubt either that there was much truth in them. Russian soldiers did rape and loot on an extensive scale. That is a fact. As an American I do not say this complacently: American soldiers looted as thoroughly, if not always as brutally, as the Russians. Americans seldom raped, but they did not need to: they had chocolate and cigarettes. The fact remains that the Russians made a bad impression on the Germans—a worse impression than did the Americans, and a very much worse impression than did the British.

That first impression need not have been fatal. There were even many Germans who were willing to say: "This hasn't been very nice but after all these men are soldiers, they have been fighting hard, they feel they are entitled to some reward, soldiers of all nations loot, and these Russians have no reason to love the Germans who killed their comrades, looted their country and raped their women."

It was the subsequent Russian actions that really confirmed the Germans in their anti-Slavic, anti-Eastern, anti-Bolshevist prejudices and hates. The Russian reparations programme—if it can be called a programme—was probably the largest factor in turning the Germans against the Russians; another factor was the close resemblance of the methods and tactics used by the Russians and the German Communists to those with which the Germans had become familiar during the Nazi period. Most Germans, corrupted as they had been by many of the nationalistic and racialistic theories of Nazism, nevertheless had a pretty healthy hatred for dictatorship by 1945—a hatred which had been much less apparent in 1933.

It is true that Germany had had no long experience of democracy comparable to that of the English, the Americans and the French; but neither had they experienced anything as efficiently dictatorial as the Nazi system, with its secret police and its iron control, exercised with the help of all the unprecedented modern methods of communication and transportation and propaganda. They learned about absolute dictatorship the hard way, and just didn't want to exchange the Nazi one for a Communist one.

Apart from the initial impression made by their troops, who were brought under discipline control fairly soon, the Russians did not make a bad start. They permitted four political parties, and these were the parties that would normally have come to the fore, as they did subsequently in western Germany. The Communist party announced that it would favour a parliamentary democracy and that the Soviet system was not suited to "present conditions" in Germany. The land reform (redistribution of the large Junker estates) was a popular measure, although there were some objections to the manner of carrying it out. It destroyed the feudal Prussian junkers caste, which had traditionally been aggressively militaristic, and reactionary in the true sense of the word. It was a social reform of the kind that took place in France after 1789. It may not have been sound economically, since the new holdings were too small for maximum efficiency; but it was good politics from the Russian point of view, and won them the allegiance at least of the class that benefited directly by it.

The Russians were also quick to get industrial production going. The Soviet zone had, in Saxony and Thuringia, the principal brown coal (lignite) fields in Germany. It lacked the hard coking coal needed for steel blast furnaces, but the coal it did have was suited to the food industries, to textile and other light industries and to electric-power generation. On the whole, the Soviet zone was the most nearly self-sufficient in Germany, with a healthy balance between medium and light industries on the one hand, and agriculture on the other. Artificial rubber was provided by the Buna plant near Halle, and gasoline was obtained from the giant Leuna synthetic petrol plant at Merseburg (which German technical ingenuity brought back into production despite the 13,000 tons of bombs the American Air Force had dropped on it, and despite the removal by the Americans, before they evacuated Saxony, of the twenty-nine top directors, managers and section chiefs).

The contradictions in Russian policy practically nullified these achievements. I have said the Russians aimed at dominating Germany. They hoped to do this through control of the German parties, and eventually the German Government in Berlin. The prospect of a strong, friendly workers' State in the heart of Europe was attractive to the Soviet mind. Yet even at the start the Russians must have had their doubts as to how far they could rely on such a State to remain friendly. This partly explains their attempts to reduce Germany to industrial impotence. Even more important, however, was their desire for reparations.

I believe it would be almost impossible to over-estimate the importance of reparations in Soviet policy. German machines and German products were needed to rebuild the Russian economy. Russian public opinion demanded it.

This may sound like a peculiar statement to Americans who are inclined to believe that public opinion in Russia doesn't count. True, it is inarticulate; nevertheless it must be taken into account by the Soviet leaders. It was particularly important for them to give the Russian people more consumer goods after so many Russian soldiers had seen that even in the war-torn and never very prosperous countries of eastern and central Europe there had been a higher standard of living than in Russia. Red Army troops had looked into the shop windows of Bucharest and Budapest and Prague and Vienna. They had entered the well-furnished houses of Berlin, and while looting curtains and dresses and shoes could not have helped wondering when these things would be as plentiful in the Soviet Union.

Americans heard little about Russia's internal problems.

They could only guess or deduce from occasional hints at the extent of the difficulties created by re-deployment and reconversion and rehabilitation. These difficulties, though unpublicized, were none the less real and tremendous; and resulted in continual pressure from Moscow on the Soviet Administration in Germany to wring more out of the German economy.

So it happened that factories which had resumed production would suddenly be closed down and their machines dismantled for shipment to Moscow or Leningrad, to the Ukraine or the Caucasus or the Urals. Towards the end of 1945 Marshal Zhukov told the German leaders in his administration that the removals were ended. Production during the last three months of the year had averaged 600,000,000 marks, which, with prices and wages frozen at pre-war levels, meant about $240,000,000, or 30 per cent of the 1938 rate. An ambitious programme of 17,000,000,000 marks was outlined for 1946 (compared with 25,000,000,000 marks in 1938). It could not be realized. Zhukov's promise that removals were ended was undoubtedly made in good faith, but in the early months of 1946 he got orders from Moscow to proceed with further removals.

I outlined the effects of these removals in an article written on April 25 of that year:

"From 70 to 80 per cent of the latest removals consist of plants devoted to purely peace-time production; in other words, of the capacity needed for the light non-war industries which the Allies have bound themselves to encourage in Germany.

"Textile factories and sugar refineries do not fall in the category from which reparations are supposed to be taken, but the Russians argue that they need these plants as replacements for those the Germans destroyed in the Soviet Union.

"Most of the current removals are taking place in Thuringia and the Prussian province of Saxony, areas that suffered relatively little from the removals of last summer and fall. Since most of the factories affected already had resumed production, industrial schedules in the zone this year have had to be revised and tens of thousands of workers suddenly face unemployment.

140

"The largest plants removed by the Russians since March 1 include the I.G. Farben chemical works at Bitterfield and at Wolfen in the province of Saxony; 50 per cent of the remaining capacity of the badly bombed Leuna synthetic gasoline plant at Merseburg; the Bayerische Stickstoffwerke at Pilteritz, near Halle, a war-time explosives plant which now produces nitrogen for fertilizers; 60 per cent of the Rudolf Sack agricultural machinery factory at Leipzig; the Lingl shoe factory at Saalfield; the ELBEO and ROGO stocking factories in the state of Saxony, and various paper, furniture, weaving and other factories.

"Twelve sugar refineries, including the large one at Tangermuende on the Elbe, also have been removed. Since there was excess sugar refining capacity in this part of Germany, the adverse effect on the food situation will be negligible. The social effects, however, will be more serious, since one-industry towns like Tangermuende face economic ruin.

"If one takes as a basis for comparison the 80 to 85 per cent of the 1938 productive capacity that was not purely for war purposes, it may be said that between 45 and 50 per cent of this capacity remains, the difference being accounted for in part by bomb damage but mainly by removals. The removals also have extended to such items as railway tracks, telephone and telegraph wires and livestock."

One need hardly stress the difficulties the Russians would naturally have in gaining the support of the German workers when the Red Army was taking away these workers' means of livelihood. Their removals of cows and farm machinery threatened to balance out their popularity with the farmers who benefited by their land reform. The lower standard of living which their removals imposed on the whole population could not help but affect their popularity among all economic groups.

In the spring of 1946 the removals stopped again, and the Germans were told that they were definitely over this time. From then on the Russians would take their reparations in the form of current production. They had already been doing this to a considerable extent, as may be seen from the following figures, provided by a German official in one of the central administrations.

	To Russians.	To Germans.
Cotton goods, metres . .	31,400,000	9,700,000
Woollen goods, metres . .	12,000,000	1,200,000
Artificial silk, metres . ,	4,100,000	500,000
Leather and cloth shoes, pairs .	1,485,000	300,000
Bicycles	5,000	0
Watches	130,000	10,000
Soap, tons	2,760	1,600
Sewing machines, tons . .	5,000	2,000
Typewriters, tons . . .	4,000	2,000

If planned production was not met, the Russian quota got priority. For instance, of a "planned" production of 28,000,000 eggs, the Russians were to take 8,000,000. The zone's hens lagged behind schedule, and laid only half the number of eggs planned. The Russians still got their 8,000,000.

The Germans were to get all but 4,000 tons of an expected potato crop of 347,000 tons; but included in the German figure were 143,000 tons for "industrial processing", meaning vodka. There was a good deal of this type of juggling with figures. For instance, Marshal Sokolovsky boasted to the German administrative leaders in his zone that out of a total production of 2,000,000,000 marks in the first quarter of 1946, only 15 per cent went for reparations. Food-processing, coal-mining and power generation were included in his figure. Genuine industrial production amounted to only about 600,000,000 marks. The coal could not very well be counted as going to the Germans, since a large part of it was used for producing reparations goods. Actually over 50 per cent of the finished goods produced, and possibly as high as 80 per cent, went to the Russians. Even the Soviet authorities did not know the exact figure because they had so many independent agencies exacting reparations that the Russians in Berlin had no clear over-all picture of what was going out.

What was clear was that the zonal economy would not support such a strain indefinitely. In order to meet quotas, the Germans had been using up stocks on hand, utilizing abandoned German Army material as a source of metals, and taking other measures that could not be continued indefinitely. The insignificant steel production of 60,000 tons a quarter did not help much. There was a shortage of spare parts for machines that broke down. The Soviet zone, like the others, would begin to suffer increasingly from the lack of economic unity in Germany.

As a substitute, the Russians proposed to set up a four-Power commission to promote interzonal trade. They were not ready to co-operate in treating Germany as an economic whole because they were unwilling to contribute the surpluses of their zone to the general economy, because they did not want to share in the financial responsibility for German imports, and because they wanted no four-Power control over or interference in the Soviet zone. They wanted to see if they could get some of the benefits of economic unity without its inconveniences and restrictive effects.

It would be pleasant to record that the Americans made no mistakes comparable to the Russian ones. Unfortunately it is impossible to do so. I have already indicated that the behaviour of individual American soldiers was not always exemplary, that the G.I. was not a very good ambassador of democracy. It is a more serious charge that the Army as an official institution is likewise open to strong criticism. The Americans did not need cows and machines; but they were often as ruthless as the Russians in taking the things they did want.

The requisitioning of houses for the use of the occupation forces was a military necessity. It was not necessary to throw the owners out in a brutal manner with half an hour's notice, letting them take only what they could gather together in that short time to whatever cellar they could find. It was not necessary to forbid them to come back to collect the potatoes stored in their cellars or the vegetables in their gardens. It may have been necessary to requisition furniture and curtains and rugs and fixtures from houses where Germans were still living, but it was done much too extensively and without proper controls.

Moreover, there was no time limit set on the requisitioning of houses. It is still going on in Berlin, so the average German there, unless he occupies a badly bombed residence, has lived for eighteen months with the haunting knowledge that the next day he might find himself on the street. It was a scandal that an American officer and his wife could live in a house of from eight to fifteen rooms in a city where the average residents were living three or four in one room. It was a scandal that for nearly a year no differentiation was made between Nazis, non-Nazis and anti-Nazis: they were all Germans and could be booted out.

The biggest scandal was the methodical looting. I do not refer to looting by individual soldiers during combat; that was understandable, though not desirable. I am talking about the people ranging from delegates to the Potsdam Conference down through colonels and majors to private soldiers, who sent back whole libraries, sets of costly china, silver—anything of value in the houses that had been requisitioned for them. The Army encouraged this kind of loot by throwing open its postal service to its personnel who could send back duty-free unlimited quantities of parcels without any control being exercised over their contents. I know personally of the case of a German intellectual who actively opposed the Nazis and spent two years in Sachsenhausen concentration camp. His house was requisitioned for an American colonel. This Colonel knew the German anti-Nazi, knew his record, became friendly with him, and promised him that he would take good care of his possessions. When the Colonel left, the house was returned to the German. He found that the better part of his priceless 10,000-volume library was gone.

The Kronberg jewel theft was a dramatic story, but it came out only because there was nobody higher than a colonel involved. Other scandals of this type, if they had been revealed, would have touched men in such high places that there would have been international repercussions.

I cannot pass from this unpleasant subject without mentioning the Berlin barter market. It is an Army-sponsored trading centre meant to curb the black market. Americans can bring cigarettes and food and other items sent from the States and trade them for anything the Germans are willing to part with. The values are all loaded in favour of the Americans. One American woman told me how a box of caramels brought her an expensive set of Dresden china. The justification offered is that on the black market there is an even greater discrepancy. But the barter market is official, and it smacks of the same type of legal looting the Nazis practised in the countries they occupied. They put an inflated value on their reichsmarks; we put an inflated value on our cigarettes. When the Nazis did it they were, quite rightly, put on trial for crimes against humanity.

All the practices I have described deserve to be condemned on moral grounds. It is no justification to say that the Germans did as bad and worse. They are being punished for what they did. The punishment should not include this kind of retaliation, which is not punishment at all, but pure exploitation. Apart from the moral issues, I cite these things to show how American policy and military government in Germany are hamstrung by the actions of the American Army. I must give one more example, this time of a different nature.

I have said that one of the principal factors in turning the Germans against the Russians was their dictatorial, secret-police *modus operandi*, too reminiscent of Nazi methods. In our ideological contest with the Russians—a contest that is going on in Germany, as all over Europe—our trump card is our championship of human rights and liberties, of the worth of the individual, the rights of man. The Russians have talking-points in their economic and social programmes, and we would do well to look to that, too. But it is our defence of man as an individual, as against the Russian conception of man as a cog in the state machine, that has won us what we have in Europe.

We cannot afford to act in violation of our own principles. It was not good, though it may be argued that it was necessary, to suspend *habeas corpus* and all the other Anglo-Saxon rights of legal protection in the case of over 100,000 interned Nazis. It was undoubtedly wrong, though again it might be argued that it was necessary, in the interests of Allied harmony, to acquiesce in the inhuman mass expulsion of over 10,000,000 human beings, largely old people, women and children, from their homes in Poland, Czechoslovakia and eastern Germany; and in the indefinite forced labour of untold millions of prisoners of war in Russia, France and England. I suggest that in view of these things most of the crimes against humanity might better have been left out of the Nuernberg indictment.

What I am proposing to attack here as inexcusable from any point of view are the activities of the American secret police in Germany, of our C.I.C. (Counter-Intelligence Corps) and C.I.D. (Criminal Investigation Division) and other hush-hush, cloak-and-dagger, amateur detective outfits. These agents repeatedly embarrassed the military government by making

145

stupid arrests whose political implications they were unable to grasp.

On July 23 John Elliott reported to the *New York Herald Tribune*:—

"Ludwig Ficker, Communist Minister of the Interior of Bavaria, who was arrested at 3 a.m. yesterday by a United States Army Officer and three soldiers, told this correspondent to-night that he was confined without food in an American prison cell at Munich for seventeen hours and questioned about his connections with the Red Army and Russian secret police.

"Ficker said that only when he had repeatedly given assurances that he had no connection with any sort of Russians was he finally released, together with three other Communists who had been arrested at the same time.

"He said the Americans had broken into his house, forced him at revolver point to get out of bed and then searched his house from attic to cellar.

"Colonel George S. Eyster (formerly Brigadier General), public relations officer of the United States Forces, European Theater, at Frankfurt on Main, said to-day that Ficker's arrest was a technical mistake and a case of mistaken identity."

Another case of "mistaken identity" occurred when C.I.D. agents showed up at the house of Jakob Kaiser, chairman of the Christian Democratic Union of the Soviet zone, at one in the morning and demanded admittance, although the house was in the British sector of Berlin. Kaiser was saved from arrest only because a representative of Ambassador Robert Murphy rushed to Kaiser's house (in answer to his telephone call) and told the would-be detectives they must be crazy and didn't know what they were doing.

These examples are sensational, but not exceptional. It was standard operating procedure for the American Gestapo, using the familiar Himmler "Nacht und Nebel" (Night and Fog) technique, to break into the houses of suspected Nazis (or Communists) in the middle of the night and whisk their victims away, leaving the families completely in the dark as to their fate. Interrogations included beating-up, deprival of food, and other third-degree methods. There were, of course, no charges preferred, no recourse to counsel allowed.

My own telephone in Berlin was tapped in 1946 in the same way as it was in 1939; the Americans used the recording apparatus obligingly left behind by the Nazis. It was over a year before the military government was able to persuade the Army to curb the activities of our G.P.U. The C.I.C. was required to notify military government prior to making arrests, to prefer charges within forty-eight hours, and to give those arrested access to counsel.

Apart from the political stupidity of "mistakenly" arresting leading German politicians, the very existence of an uncontrolled, irresponsible American secret police is a negation of American principles. It is not the way to teach the Germans democracy and it is not the way to demonstrate to them the superiority of our system to that of the Russians. In the midst of an ideological contest America cannot afford to blunt its own best weapons.

X

WORKERS OF GERMANY, UNITE

News Picture

Berlin, March 1. Berlin Social Democrats turned today against their party leadership with an overwhelming vote of opposition to the proposed merger with the German Communist party.

In this city's stormiest political meeting since the war, Otto Grotewohl, chairman of the Social Democratic party and a leader in the merger movement, was shouted down by 2,000 delegates whose spokesman made it clear they believed Grotewohl was acting under Russian pressure.

The delegates were angered by what they termed the undemocratic tactics of the central committee, and specifically by its efforts to railroad the meeting into approving the official resolution for an immediate merger. The resolution was defeated by 5 to 1. With a show of hands the delegates had already approved by a similar margin another resolution calling for a secret-ballot plebiscite of all party members in the Russian zone on whether to dissolve the party and link with the Communists.

GERMAN REDS INTENSIFY BID TO SOCIALISTS
SOCIAL DEMOCRATIC FOES OF MERGER MOBILIZE FORCES IN NON
    RUSSIAN SECTORS
. . . BERLINER HOOTED AS HE QUESTIONS LEFTIST MERGER . . .
LEADERS SEEK MERGER OF TWO GERMAN PARTIES . . . FULL ELEC-
TIONS AUTHORIZED IN RUSSIAN ZONE MERGER OF THE COMMUNIST
AND SOCIALIST PARTIES WILL PRECEDE BALLOTING . . . MERGER
DISPUTE GROWS HOTTER IN GERMAN PARTY. . . .
GERMAN EDITOR SAYS HIS PARTY IMITATES HITLER
OUSTED 4 DAYS AGO FOE OF MERGING WITH REDS ATTACKS SOCIAL
    DEMOCRATS
. . . PARTY IN BERLIN URGES BOYCOTT OF MERGER VOTE . . . US
SUPPORTS GERMAN PARTY POLL ON MERGER . . . GERMAN PARTYS
VOTE ON MERGER SET FOR TODAY . . . BERLIN SOCIAL DEMOCRATS
BAN JOINING REDS . . . BERLIN SOCIALIST FOES OF MERGER PLAN A
MEETING . . . SOCIALIST RED UNITY PARTY IS SET UP IN BERLIN . . .
REDS SOCIALISTS IN RUSSIAN ZONE TO MERGE TODAY

One morning in April of 1946 subscribers to the newspaper *Das Volk*, at that time the organ of the Social Democratic party in the Soviet zone, read on the front page of that day's paper the bold headline: "NUR NOCH EINE PARTEI", which may be translated "Only one party now". *Das Volk* was announcing the merger of the Social Democratic and Communist parties, and meant that there was one party where there had been two. Many Social Democratic readers, having had enough experience during the Nazi era of "only one party", must have thought uneasily: "Isn't this where I came in?"

Germans of varying political creeds probably wondered whether the headline was prophetic and whether the two bourgeois parties in the Soviet zone—the Christian Democrats and the Liberal Democrats—would be merged with the Communists or suppressed, leaving "only one party". Such fears were not allayed by statements like one made at that time by a leader of the new Socialist Unity party, who said: "We will expand beyond the framework of the Party and will become a real people's party and people's movement."

But the Russians were not interested in creating a monopoly party in eastern Germany merely for the sake of imposing Soviet political forms on their occupation zone. What they were interested in was creating a strong, united workers' party that would gain a clear majority in the Soviet zone and would then spread its control throughout Germany. They hoped in this way to control the future German Government, thereby insuring that Germany's orientation would be pro-Soviet.

When the Nazi regime collapsed, the opposition leaders came out of hiding, out of the concentration camps, and out of prudent inactivity, and began to reorganize. They did this all over Germany, even before political parties were legalized. The most active, the most courageous, the most intelligent of the leaders had for the most part been liquidated. Many of those who had survived the concentration camps had had their spirit broken there.

In the Soviet zone the Communists enjoyed a big advantage in this respect, because the Red Army brought in its wake several thousand Communist leaders and organizers who had fled the Nazis and lived in exile in the Soviet Union for up to twelve years. While there they had been carefully schooled and indoctrinated. These men not only set to work to reconstruct the Communist party, but were placed in key administrative positions throughout the zone. Non-communists were also given posts, but the Communists, being more active, more purposeful, better organized, and strategically placed, were dominant.

However, they lacked popular support. The preference and advantages they were given by the occupation Power were politically harmful to them because they were identified in the public mind with the occupation. They lost supporters, real or potential, every time a German house was looted or a German woman raped by a Red Army soldier. The Russians soon began to look around for a way of reaching a broader segment of the German population. The idea of a merger of the two Marxist parties seemed a "natural".

The German working-class movement had twice been split, first in 1914 over the issue of war credits, and again after the First World War when the more revolutionary Communists broke away from the Social Democrats, with whom they differed on the very important question of ways and means of achieving an identical goal: the socialist State. The split and the consequent *"Bruderkampf"* (fratricidal strife) had weakened the workers, and had undoubtedly played into the hands of the Nazis.

Both Communists and Social Democrats agreed that without this split Hitler probably would not have been able to come to power. At the end of the second war there was a general tendency to recognize the foolishness of this split, to forget past quarrels and forgive past mistakes, and to work together to prevent a come-back by the "reactionaries". In the concentration camps there had been serious talk of forming a united workers' party as soon as the war was over.

The Social Democrats proposed that since both party organizations were practically non-existent and would have to be built up again from scratch, it would be a good idea to start right off building the new united party. Their Communist comrades were inclined to agree—until they got out of the camps and discovered that the "line" was that the old parties should be reconstituted and that ideologies would have to be "clarified" before a single party could be formed. The Social Democrats interpreted this as meaning that the Com-

150

munists wanted to get their own organization firmly established so that they would not lose their identity, but would remain a kind of party within a party.

For several months the Communists seemed to be in no hurry about fusing with the Socialists. On July 29, 1945, I had an interview with Wilhelm Pieck, the snowy-haired, mild-mannered seventy-year-old leader of the Communists. He told me that the idea of a united Marxist party had not yet been put up to the Social Democratic leaders, and that many of them were probably not yet ready for it. He believed it might take years for such a party to emerge, and suggested that a long process of education would be necessary.

The Social Democrats, despite their initial rebuff, were for close co-operation with the Communists, and hoped a merger could eventually be brought about. However, they wanted time to observe the Communists' actions and make sure the latter did not use the merger as a way of capturing the Social Democratic party. Two days after the Pieck interview I saw Otto Grotewohl and Max Fechner, the two top Social Democratic leaders.

They told me:

"The merger of the two parties should not result from decisions or orders of the party leadership, but should develop out of work together. Agreement on ideological questions must result from discussions and joint demonstrations. In this way the division into two parties will come to seem superfluous and the merger of the Social Democratic party and the Communist party into one large workers' party will follow inevitably from the growing community of views and actions."

The formation of joint working committees and of a Socialist–Communist bloc within the four-Power bloc of anti-Fascist parties in Berlin was well in line with this policy. So was the meeting, on December 20 and 21, 1945, of the thirty top leaders of the two parties to discuss preparations for an eventual merger. Even at this time the Communists did not seem to think it would come about in less than a year.

The Socialists, for their part, were already beginning to entertain the gravest doubts of the possibility that the Communists would ever work with them sincerely and loyally. They did not like the idea of carrying out the merger first only

151

in the Soviet zone, because they felt this would give the Communists a chance to dominate the new party, that it would split the Social Democratic party as a national organization, and that it might also help split Germany. Furthermore, they wanted to wait until after elections had been held, because they were sure they were stronger than the Communists, and they wanted the distribution of top positions in the new party to reflect this strength. The Communists proposed that the key posts be divided on a fifty-fifty basis.

Grotewohl took the occasion of the December 20 "Conference of the Sixty" to voice the doubts and fears felt by the Social Democrats. He expounded ten points which expressed "the anxieties that have grown in us in the last six months". In his words they were:

"1. The Communist party enjoys a considerably greater and more active support from the Soviet occupation power than the Social Democratic party.

"2. The Communist party often does not act in the spirit of the democratic principles it proclaims and of the agreed co-operation.

"3. These departures from the spirit and letter of our agreements have resulted in increasing doubt on the part of Social Democratic officials and followers in the sincerity of the Communists' desire for unity except on the basis of their own predominance.

"4. We declare that preparations for a merger can go ahead only if an end is put to the favoured position of the Communist party and if pressure on the Social Democratic party and on individual Social Democrats ceases.

"5. We declare further that we are prepared to withdraw our representatives from all responsible administrative positions if the above prerequisites for co-operation and unity are not fulfilled.

"6. We are prepared to consider a common election programme and join lists of candidates in the event of elections only after the fulfilment of these prerequisites.

"7. We cannot and will not make any binding declaration about co-operation, election programmes or joint lists in the English, American and French zones before the formation of a national Social Democratic party and the election of its officials at a Reich party congress.

"8. With regard to a common election programme and joint lists in the Soviet zone and Berlin, we feel this issue cannot be decided in one zone any more than can the merger of the two parties. This would endanger the political unity of Germany and the unity of the Social Democratic party throughout the Reich. There are also important tactical considerations against joint lists of candidates. (He was referring to the belief of the Social Democrats that they could poll more votes than the Communists, and could therefore elect more candidates by running separately.)

"9. We reiterate our willingness to work closely with the Communist party in building a parliamentary democratic republic. We are committed to a policy which will eliminate the mistakes and weaknesses of the past.

"10. We take the view that the two parties must make it their aim to dissolve themselves at the appropriate time in order to form a new, united, independent German workers' party, based on the principle of inner party democracy."

Six months of collaboration quite clearly had not brought the two parties any closer to that agreement on ideological questions which was to make the division into two parties seem superfluous. They were, in fact, farther apart than they had been in those June days when the Communist party, in its first public declaration of policy, had announced:

"We are of the opinion that it would be wrong to force the Soviet system on Germany because this would not correspond to the present stage of development (Entwicklungsbedingungen) in Germany. We believe the decisive interests of the German people in the present situation require the formation of an anti-fascist, democratic regime, a parliamentary-democratic republic with all democratic rights and freedom for the people."

The Social Democrats had been willing to accept this declaration at face value, even though the phrases " present stage of development" and "in the present situation" suggested the likelihood that the Communists might, at some later stage, be prepared to throw over the parliamentary-democratic republic and abolish the democratic rights and freedoms of the

153

people. The Communists' actions soon convinced most of the Social Democratic leaders that tactical considerations alone had prompted the Communist declaration.

The general public knew little about these differences between the two parties. Grotewohl's remarks were not printed even in his own party newspaper, which was, of course, controlled and censored by the Red Army. This paper carried only the text of a joint declaration filled with generalities about closer collaboration and work towards unity. The merger was left in the indefinite future. The Social Democrats having turned down the idea of joint lists of candidates in elections, the declaration merely stated that the two parties would have common election *programmes*. This was a concession that did not give away very much.

The matter rested there for about six weeks. As late as January 25, Grotewohl assured a non-Socialist friend that the Social Democrats would never agree to a merger except on the basis of a decision by a national party congress. In the early days of February he began to be subjected to Russian pressure. He was called to Karlshorst, the headquarters of Soviet Military Government, and told that the Russians wanted the merger to go through quickly and that he would be acting against the interests of the German people if he opposed it. They explained that a united workers' party would give the Russians increased confidence in the Germans, and would therefore result in a reduction in reparations, in higher food rations and in a shortening of the occupation.

The sudden Russian wish for speed was probably connected with the results of the elections in the American zone on January 20 and 27. The Communist party made a poor showing there, getting only about 3 per cent of the votes. It had done equally poorly in the Austrian elections. These results could be partially discounted on the grounds that both Austria and Bavaria are predominantly Catholic lands where the Communists have never shown great strength. Furthermore, voting in the American zone was only in rural communities where the conservative Christian Democratic Union (Christian Social Union in Bavaria) was strongest. Nevertheless, the poor showing made by the Communists could not be entirely explained away in this manner. The Russians knew it.

It was becoming clear that the peoples of Central Europe, far from being in a revolutionary mood at the end of the war, were inclined to reject Soviet-backed Communism. The one exception was Czechoslovakia, where the Russian troops had been better behaved than in other countries and were rather quickly withdrawn; where the memory of the Munich betrayal by the Western democracies was still alive; and where the people believed a pro-Soviet policy would be their best way of keeping their democratic liberties.

The Russians did not want to lag too far behind the Americans in holding elections in Germany. But they knew that a defeat for the German Communist party would be a slap at the occupation Power. The Russians believed such a defeat was indicated if the Communists and Social Democrats put up separate lists, but that the Communists and Social Democrats together could get a clear majority. If they campaigned as one party it would not be apparent how many of the votes were cast for each group. The united party would be controlled by the Communists, and at least half of the candidates would be Communists. They decided to push through the fusion by May 1st, the traditional international Labour Day, and hold the first elections in their zone in June.

Grotewohl, acting under this pressure, went to Hanover and on February 8 had a conference with Kurt Schumacher, who was unofficially recognized as the political leader of the Social Democrats in western Germany. He proposed a national congress of the Social Democratic party to decide the question of the merger. Schumacher, an anti-Communist whose stubborn fanaticism blinded him to his party's best interests, said such a congress could not be held until the zones were abolished.

It was a stupid refusal, because at a national congress the representatives of the western Social Democrats would have been in the majority, and the congress would not have been subjected to Soviet pressure, as was the case with the Soviet zonal congress which Grotewohl proposed as an alternative. Schumacher may have believed the occupying Powers would not have permitted a national congress. Both the British and American military governments shortly made it clear that this was not true as far as they were concerned. Only the French, with their hypersensitive fear of any kind of control organization in Germany, were opposed to it. A veto on the merger by a national congress would have given Grotewohl a good excuse for not acceding to the Russian demands. Lacking this "out", he decided to go ahead with the merger in the Soviet zone alone.

He returned to Berlin, and on February 10 astounded his own party followers by announcing publicly at a trades union congress that he would call a rally of Social Democrats from the Russian zone and Berlin to take up the question of immediate fusion with the Communists. On the same occasion, Walter Ulbricht, the executive secretary of the Communist party, who was, much more than Pieck, the real leader of the Communists, and whose advice had been followed by the Russians when they decided on a quick merger, announced categorically that "the Communists and Social Democrats will be fused before May 1".

The following day there was a meeting of the Central Committee of the Social Democratic party. Delegates from the provincial organizations in the Soviet zone were present. A proposal for immediate merger was first voted down, but later approved after the provincial delegates, who were naturally under greater pressure than the leaders in Berlin, announced that if necessary they would ignore the Central Committee and carry out the fusion in their separate provinces. This would have left the Central Committee hanging in the air.

Grotewohl, a man of considerable ability and intelligence but of weak character, was now prepared to proceed with the merger. He felt he had been let down not only by the western Social Democrats but also by the western Powers. This was not entirely true. The British were prepared to give the Social Democrats considerable unofficial support. They and the Americans may have been somewhat slow in announcing that they would not oppose a national party congress; they were probably taken unawares by the sudden Russian decision to push the merger through quickly.

The Americans did not believe in favouring one party over another. They felt this was undemocratic, and would, moreover, boomerang by placing the favoured party in an unfavourable light in the eyes of the electorate. While the Russians encouraged the political leaders whom they supported by giving them preferential treatment, inviting them to lavish banquets and so forth, the Americans scrupulously refrained from doing anything of the sort. Clay would not even entertain the members of his Laenderrat to lunch—not, he said, because of a feeling against fraternization, but because it would smack of bribery and would harm the German leaders politically by making them look like collaborationists.

On the other hand, the Americans were not prepared to recognize any fusion which was not democratically brought about, any fusion by party leaders not endorsed by the party membership. They could thus block, and did subsequently block for all practical purposes, such a fusion in Berlin, where there was effective four-Power control. They were not in a position to block it in the Russian zone.

Grotewohl was mistaken if he thought his decision and that of the party Central Committee would be considered automatically binding by the party membership. In all the Russian zone there was little open opposition. Leaders who opposed the merger were quietly removed from their administrative and party positions. They were branded as reactionaries and pro-Fascists. The few who had the courage to speak up disappeared mysteriously, usually ending up in the concentration camps of Buchenwald and Sachsenhausen. Hermann Brill, a Social Democrat who was in Buchenwald when the camp was liberated, and was installed as President of Thuringia by the Americans, was considered politically suspect by the Russians and removed. He went to Berlin to become an advisor to the Office of Military Government (U.S.). In factories and administrative offices throughout the zone personnel checks were made and individuals were vetted as to their political attitude. If they were not for the party (not the Nazi party this time but the Socialist Unity party) they were likely to forfeit their chances of advancement, perhaps lose their jobs, and be put in an inferior food-ration category.

In Berlin the pressures were harder to apply. They were there, too, because it was easy to whisk a man out of the American or French sector into a jail in the Russian zone. Also, many Germans were not sure how long the Western Allies would stay in Berlin; they feared to compromise themselves politically. Many Germans preferred to stay away from politics entirely: they had seen how the anti-Nazis suffered during the Hitler period, how the Nazis suffered under the occupation, and preferred not to commit themselves to any group lest it, too, find itself in the political doghouse at some future time.

There were many, nevertheless, particularly among the secondary leaders of the Social Democrats, who had the courage to speak up. When, on March 1, Grotewohl tried to railroad a merger resolution through a meeting of Berlin party functionaries, he was shouted down by the assembly despite the fact that the meeting was held in the State Opera House in the Russian sector of the city, that Soviet political observers were present, and that nearly half the delegates lived in the Russian sector. These delegates made speeches which showed real courage, and were a heartening evidence that there were at least some German groups which understood and valued democracy and were willing to fight for it. Grotewohl, exasperated by this revolt, said angrily: "I know you don't want to hear my agruments. But in that case I don't know why you bothered to come here at all."

In the subsequent discussion a delegate stood up and said: "I will tell Comrade Grotewohl why we bothered to come here. We came to save democracy in our party."

The revolting delegates, led by Franz Neumann, mayor of the city district of Reinickendorf in the French sector, voted that a merger should take place only after a plebiscite of the party membership in the Russian zone. This marked the beginning of a six weeks' long, bitter political battle—the first battle in the struggle for Berlin. The Russians had hoped to sweep Berlin along with the Russian zone in the merger movement. The political importance of the city as Germany's traditional capital was out of proportion to its 3,000,000 inhabitants. As Berlin went, it was felt on all sides, so would Germany eventually go. The British and Americans insisted that Berlin could not be regarded as an appendage to the Soviet zone, that it was under four-Power control and should be treated as a kind of fifth zone. It was pointed out to the Russians that unanimous four-Power approval must be obtained before any new party, or merger of old parties, could be recognized there.

After his humiliation in the Opera House at the hands of the Neumann group, Grotewohl turned savagely on his former followers. He used methods which the Communists themselves would have hesitated to employ. He announced that a plebiscite in the Russian zone was unnecessary because the party there was solidly for the merger. The plebiscite in Berlin, scheduled for March 31, had to be provisionally accepted; but in a confidential letter to Lieutenant-General Feodor Bokov, Zhukov's political advisor, Grotewohl asked for Russian help in his campaign against the plebiscite. He told the Russian general that a plebiscite in Berlin was "undesirable" in view of the widespread opposition to the merger in Berlin and the unfavourable effect such a plebiscite might have in western Germany when the results were published. He asked that forty tons of newsprint be made available so that Berlin could be plastered with leaflets and flooded with pamphlets in a vast propaganda campaign against the plebiscite. He asked further that motor vehicles and fuel be placed at the disposal of party leaders. He began expelling dissident leaders and disbanding local party branches that held meetings of protest. He excluded his opponents from party conferences by issuing special passes.

The dissident Social Democrats had no newspaper in Berlin, so the American-licensed *Der Tagesspiegel* opened its columns to them. Karl Gormer, managing editor of Grotewohl's paper *Das Volk*, finding that his own paper would not print his articles, used *Der Tagesspiegel* to address Grotewohl and the other members of the Central Committee. He wrote:

"On May 3, 1945, one day after the liberation of Berlin by the Russians, three Gormers—my sons and I—rode around Berlin on bicycles, looking for Social Democrats. The results were meagre at first, but we did not give up. Then, in the middle of May, the first foundations for the resurrection of the Social Democratic party and its traditions were laid in my home. You of the central committee, except for Fechner, were then unknown to me and to many others.

"At that time I was one of those who was entrusted with building up the workers' press, and later when you came along you were kind enough to confirm me in my position. (The Central Committee was self-constituted, not elected.) But you are in error if you believe this puts me under obligation to follow you where an upright comrade cannot follow.

"*You were entrusted by us with the fulfilment of an important mission ; you were to build a bridge to the east. But what did you do? You built a wall against the west.*

"You are mistaken if you believe we called you to be the leaders of the German workers. You have learned nothing in the last twelve years because if you had you would not imitate Hitler in so many things. For instance, if someone permits himself to have a different opinion from you he falls under suspicion. You expel and exclude without having any right to do so.

"Because after twelve years of National Socialist tyranny in Germany the Communist party does not find fertile soil for a new tyranny, you want to enter into a political marriage with doctrinaires, whom we reject as leaders of the workers even as we reject you. We have not forgotten that after 1918 Pieck and Ulbricht did everything to split the workers. Often enough they stood shoulder to shoulder with the National Socialists against us. We don't need a new party because the party which to-day enjoys the confidence of the broadest masses of the people is the Social Democratic party."

Three days before the date set for the plebiscite, Grotewohl announced that since plebiscites were undemocratic (sic) the question of the merger would not be decided at the plebiscite, but at a subsequent party congress. He urged the party membership to abstain from voting. The next day Major-General Ray W. Barker, the American member of the Berlin Kommandatura, issued a statement saying the United States could recognize no merger which was not "freely demanded by a majority of the party members concerned rather than by a group of party leaders". He said he was "seriously concerned" that the plebiscite should be carried out democratically, and was satisfied that it represented "an honest attempt by party members to express their views".

On the morning of the plebiscite Red Army officers closed the polls in the eight city districts of the Soviet sector. In the twelve sectors where there was balloting 72 per cent of those entitled to vote went to the polls, and of those who voted 85 per cent opposed "an immediate merger". Over 70 per cent voted in favour of an alliance with the Communists which would "ensure co-operation and prevent fratricidal strife". The wording of the two questions on the ballot was designed to give the voters a chance to oppose immediate merger without placing themselves in the position of opposing the unity of the working class.

The official Social Democratic and Communist Press interpreted the results of the plebiscite as a victory for the merger. Since those who favoured the fusion had been instructed to abstain from voting, all abstentions (including those of nearly half the party members who lived in the Russian sector and had no chance to vote) were counted as votes for the merger.

What the Communists really thought was shown by the remark of one of their Berlin leaders who was at the Social Democratic party headquarters when the results came in; he told a pro-merger Social Democratic leader: "You have lost the battle for Berlin."

The next step was to pack the party congress which, by the ruling of the Central Committee, was to make the decision on the merger. This was done by declaring that all party officials who failed to "declare their support of working class unity" could no longer hold positions in the party. Thus all merger opponents would automatically be excluded from the congress and the vote would necessarily be unanimous. This naturally precipitated a split, and there were two party congresses, one voting against the merger and the other for it.

It was now up to the Allied Kommandatura to decide which group it would recognize. As might be expected, the Russian member favoured recognizing the S.E.D. (Sozialistische Einheitspartei Deutschlands). The Russians realized by this time that their decision to push through the fusion had been a political error, since the attitude of the Berlin Social Democrats, and the publicity given to it, had made it clear to everyone in Germany that it was a forced merger and that members in the Soviet zone would also have opposed it if they had been able to do so.

The Russians had gone too far to be able to back down gracefully. They were willing to compromise, however. General Kotikov, the Soviet member of the Berlin Kommandatura, proposed, therefore, that both the S.E.D. and the S.P.D. be recognized as legal in Berlin. This was just what the British and American political officers had been hoping for, because they believed that in any free elections the S.P.D. would win. But the French and British commandants, being unpolitically minded, got their signals crossed, and opposed the Soviet compromise proposal. Kotikov, who had expected ready acceptance, angrily and quite justly accused them of not being conversant with their own Governments' viewpoints. The matter had to be referred to the Allied Control Authority. There was no slip-up there, and the compromise was accepted, elections being set for October. The results of these elections showed that the S.E.D. was really little more than the Communist party under another name.

It did not even do as well as the pre-Hitler Communist party had done in Berlin, where in 1932 it was the strongest single party, getting more votes than either the Social Democratic or the National Socialist party. In Berlin's first post-war election, which amounted to a plebiscite in which Berliners were asked: "Do you favour Western democracy or Eastern communism?", only one-fifth of the electorate voted for the Russian-sponsored party. The Socialist Unity party, supposedly combining the strength of the two working-class parties, got only 20 per cent of the votes (32 per cent in the Soviet sector, but as low as 7 per cent in some of the western districts).

The Social Democratic party, with 49 per cent of the votes, just missed a clear majority over the other three parties combined. It did get over 50 per cent of the ballots in the three western sectors, and even in the Soviet sector it got 43 per cent of the votes. The Social Democrats were the leading party in every one of the twenty city districts or boroughs. The Socialist Unity party ran third to the Christian Democratic Union, which got 22 per cent of the votes, while the other "bourgeois" party, the Liberal Democrats, got only 9 cent.

Berlin had voted overwhelmingly for democracy (in contrast to 1933 when it voted for dictatorship). It had also voted for the Western Powers as opposed to the Russians, and so unambiguously that it was slightly embarrassing to the Western Powers themselves who must continue to work with the Russians in governing Berlin. One important practical result of the election was that the Communists, who had controlled about 80 per cent of the top posts in the city administration, would henceforth control only 20 per cent of them. Within the limits of Allied tolerance, the Social Democrats could run the city by combining with any one of the three other parties for a clear majority.

These election results did not come as a complete surprise. The weakness of the Socialist Unity party had been apparent long before it was statistically demonstrated. The Soviet zone elections were postponed from June to September because a reverse was feared. When they were held, the S.E.D. managed to get only a slim majority over the combined C.D.U. (Christian Democratic Union) and L.D.P. (Liberal Democratic Party), even though the elections were not fair as we understand fair elections.

There was no evidence that the secrecy of the ballot was violated or that the count was false; but the S.E.D. had every advantage in the campaign. It had a practical monopoly of the Press. It got paper for posters and leaflets in the ratio of about 1,000 to 1; and its advantage in other facilities such as buildings, vehicles and gasoline was similarly disproportionate.

The bourgeois parties were unable, because of technical obstructions, to put up candidates in most of the rural districts so they were able to reach only about 75 per cent of the voters. In the large cities of Leipzig and Dresden, where they could compete on more nearly even terms, the C.D.U. and L.D.P. together polled more votes than the S.E.D., although in 1932 these cities of "Red Saxony" had given the two working-class parties, the S.P.D. and K.P.D., over 50 per cent of the votes. Thus the united workers' party did not do as well as the two workers' parties running separately might have been expected to do. Many Social Democrats, following the instructions of their Berlin leaders, cast invalid ballots of protest. Some threw their votes to the C.D.U. and the L.P.D. The results in the Berlin elections give a fair indication of what would have happened in really free elections in the Soviet zone.

Russian hopes that the S.E.D. would sweep Germany were shattered by its inability to win a clear-cut victory even in their own zone. This failure naturally had an effect on overall Russian policy. The Russians were confronted by hard facts, and facts, as Lenin once said, are stubborn things.

In April the slogan of the Soviet sponsored party was: "The Elbe is no boundary for the S.E.D." It was to sweep across zonal frontiers and capture the west. In August, S.E.D. leaders were saying: "It is too early to break down the zonal boundaries because we cannot let the eastern zone be contaminated by reactionary ideas and influences from the west." The S.E.D. had gone on the defensive.

The Russians had given the German Communists reason to believe that a victory for the S.E.D. in the elections would be followed by a revision of the eastern frontiers, that Germany would get back some of the land that had been put under Polish administration. If Russia could count on a friendly Germany, it could afford a larger, stronger, united Germany.

163

The Poles would be disappointed, but the Polish bridge could be held in spite of that if the German bridgehead were secure.

The eastern frontiers were an election issue, and the S.E.D. undoubtedly got many votes from Germans who thought an S.E.D. victory would mean a return of some of the lost territories. It did not get enough votes to satisfy the Russians. And immediately after these elections Molotov took his stand against a revision of the eastern frontiers. In answer to Byrnes, who had said at Stuttgart that the Potsdam boundaries were not final, Molotov declared in an interview with a Polish journalist that they merely awaited formal ratification at the peace conference.

The Russians had decided for the time being at least that they could not count on holding the bridgehead and must secure the bridge. They sacrificed the German Communists to the Polish Communists as brutally as they had sacrificed the French Communists to the German Communists two months earlier, by opposing separation of the Ruhr and Rhineland from Germany.

Elections in the four zones of Germany indicated that if post-war Germany were united, there would be two major parties: the S.P.D. and the C.D.U. The S.P.D. would be the main workers' party. For this reason the Russians might have to decide to make a truce with the S.P.D. unless it were willing to split Germany and settle for the eastern half—or rather less than half. As long as the Ruhr and Rhineland remained a part of Germany, the Russians would be reluctant to give up their voice in the control of that vital area, and would be inclined to leave the door open to a united Germany, to maintain the machinery of quadripartite government (actual quadripartite government never having existed).

The S.P.D. would probably favour such a truce. It had always been willing to co-operate with the Communists. It had conceived its rôle as that of a bridge between east and west. It had not been happy about having been jockeyed into an anti-Soviet position during the merger dispute. The Russians could not fail to realize that in trying to unite the German working class they had effectively split it.

The S.P.D. needed a positive programme. It needed an appeal broader and more constructive than that of opposition to Communism. For that the voters could turn to the more conservative parties. The Social Democrats were still Socialists.

In ideology they had not clearly formulated their differences from the Communists, had not stated how much of the rigid Marxist dogma they were prepared to throw overboard. If they could gain the confidence of the Russians without being dominated by them, they might seize the leadership in forming a Germany that would be neither anti-Russian nor yet in the Russian sphere, that would be both socialistic and democratic.

The Christian Democratic Union, the second large party in Germany, is a heterogeneous amalgam. It is the successor to the old Catholic Centre party, but it is also more than that. The post-war party was determined not to be sectarian; it wanted to appeal to Protestants as well as Catholics. By organizing in the Soviet zone, it was entering an area where, because there is no large Catholic population, the Centre party had never had any strength (it used to get between 1 and 2 per cent of the votes there). In the first post-war elections in the Russian zone the C.D.U. came out third, slightly behind the L.D.P., but it had definitely attained major party status. In Bavaria, where it called itself the Christian Social Union or C.S.U., in Wuerttemberg-Baden, in the French zone and in large parts of the Rhineland, the C.D.U. was the strongest party. Its weakness, indeed, lay in its size. Like the Republicans and Democratic parties in the United States, its followers represented many shades of opinion and many economic interests.

Jakob Kaiser, the leader of the party in Berlin and the Russian zone, is a Catholic trades union leader, a believer in Socialism, but a Christian Socialism as opposed to a Marxist Socialism. Like the Social Democrats, he opposes the dicta-torial, anti-democratic aspect of Communism. In an election speech at Potsdam he read to a meeting a letter to workers in a certain factory who were told they would be given time off from two to four in the afternoon. Walter Ulbricht, the Com-munist leader, would be speaking at that time and they would be expected to march together to the demonstration. Giving the workers "time off" but requiring their attendance at a political rally was a well-known Nazi practice. Kaiser remarked: "There is only one thing missing in this letter: what is it?" The delighted crowd shouted: "Heil Hitler!"

Kaiser has this advantage over the Social Democrats: that while they oppose many of the logical manifestations of Marxism, they cling to the Marxist label, and have been unable as yet to clarify their stand philosophically. Kaiser has had less trouble in reconciling Socialism with Christianity.

The second Berlin leader of the C.D.U. is Ernst Lemmer, a non-Catholic, a liberal, a former journalist of the Democratic party. Lemmer is a better speaker than Kaiser, has a more flexible mind and is superior at diplomacy—an invaluable asset in a position where diplomacy must be used in frequent contact with the Russians. Like the more astute of the Social Democrats, Lemmer would like to see his party become a bridge between east and west. Over a bottle of vodka he once told a Russian political officer: "The S.E.D. will be a great mass party, but as a bridge between the Russian and German peoples it will still be too narrow." The Russian caught on immediately and said earnestly: "Yes, yes, C.D.U. will also be a great bridge."

There are Christian Democrats in western Germany, like Mueller in Munich, who are not too far from Kaiser and Lemmer in their views. There are others farther to the right. A conservative like Adenauer believes the Russian zone is lost to the C.D.U. and to Germany, and dreams of a revival of Charlemagne's empire by a union of western Germany with France. To such men Lemmer shows the map of Germany and says what they are proposing to abandon is much more than the East-Elbian lands, since the Elbe runs through the middle of the Russian zone, and the Weser and the Main (a tributary of the Rhine) have their sources there.

There are men in the C.D.U. even farther to the right than Adenauer. I have mentioned Schaeffer of Bavaria, who was finally excluded from political life by the American military government. In the British zone, men like Schroeter in Schleswig-Holstein are still tolerated: Schroeter belonged to the now illegal German Nationalist party, the party of the Junkers and heavy industrialists, of Hugenberg, who helped Hitler to power (but was protected by the British for over a year).

The Liberal Democratic party is the only one which is openly and unequivocally pro-capitalist. Like the C.D.U., it has attracted Germans who formerly supported the anti-democratic chauvinistic parties of the extreme right. These parties being illegal now, their adherents gravitate to the most conservative remaining parties, the C.D.U., the L.D.P., and, in the British zone, a number of regional parties with separatist programmes. Paradoxically the conservative L.D.P., the party of private enterprise, made its best showing in the Soviet zone, where it garnered the conservative vote that in the Catholic areas of the west and south went more completely to the C.D.U., as well as part of the workers' vote that would have been given to the S.P.D. had this party been permitted to put up candidates.

The weakness of all parties lies in their lack of high-quality leadership, a sad inheritance from the Nazi system of concentration camps, political murders and repression. This lack of leadership is reflected in the absence of clear programmes, although this is also partly the result of the circumstance that the German nation is not yet in a position to determine its own future, and that consequently no party cares to take the responsibility for a programme it does not have the power to carry out. The C.D.U. will have a hard time reconciling the socialistic tendencies of its Berlin leaders with the clericalism and regionalism of the Bavarians and the often reactionary conservation of those in the British zone.

In the S.P.D., Neumann in Berlin has new ideas and a persuasive way of expressing them; for him democracy and Socialism are equal values, and he makes them the basis for a constructive programme, while pointing out frankly that neither Socialism nor democracy can work unless the Allies give them a chance. Neumann shows promise of developing into a political leader of real stature. Unfortunately Schumacher, the recognized leader of the Social Democrats in the west, is a narrow-minded pedant who has little to offer beyond a party patriotism that is more interested in justifying the actions of pre-1933 Social Democracy than in dealing with the realities of a new era.

The S.E.D. has Grotewohl, whose character has been sufficiently indicated, and Ulbricht, a Communist of great energy and demagogic qualities, with the "peasant cleverness" (to use a German phrase) of a Hitler, and a vast amount of unscrupulousness, ruthlessness and plain dishonesty. The S.E.D. is of course tied to Soviet policy, and is not really a German party at all. Its Russian sponsors have succeeded in depriving it of most of its appeal to the German workers by their removals of machinery and to the German nationalists by their amputation of eastern Germany.

XI

THE RUSSIAN–BRITISH CLASH

O N the afternoon of May 22, 1945, I landed on the airfield of
Flensburg, in Schleswig-Holstein, a few miles from the Danish
border. The war had been over two weeks, but we found
officers and soldiers of the German Army and Luftwaffe
wearing all their insignia, saluting each other, driving staff
cars, and in general acting in such a way that I got the
uncanny feeling that the war was still on and that I was some-
where behind the German lines.

I had come with a dozen other correspondents on an Army-
sponsored trip whose object was not disclosed to us ahead of
time. We knew that the German General Staff and the
Government of Karl Doenitz, the admiral who succeeded
Hitler as Fuehrer, had been in the Flensburg area when the
war ended. We were told that there was a S.H.A.E.F. control
ship in the harbour. It was controlling the German Government and the O.K.W. (Oberkommando der Wehrmacht),
which we were surprised to learn were still functioning. I
noted that in order to telephone from the airfield to the liner
Patria, which was the S.H.A.E.F. ship, we had to be passed
through the O.K.W. switchboard.

On board the ship we were "briefed" by the Director of
Military Intelligence, a British brigadier. He said it was
planned to abolish the O.K.W. and the German Government
in the morning. Doenitz, General Jodl and Admiral von
Friedeburg would be invited aboard ship in the morning,
then told they were under arrest. At the same time British
troops supported by tanks would move into the O.K.W. compound and take it over. Military aircraft would be overhead
and a few naval craft would be lying offshore. This was presumably to dramatize the action, since there was no likelihood
of resistance, certainly not anything that would require the use
of tanks and planes and ships.

Some of the correspondents wondered why the Nazi Government and Supreme Command had been permitted to continue
so long in existence. We did not know at the time that General
Eisenhower, who still commanded the British and French as

well as the American forces, had instructions to "search out, arrest and hold . . . Adolf Hitler, his chief Nazi associates . . . all General Staff Corps officers . . . the leading officials of all ministries and other high political officials". But it did seem peculiar that the Nazi Government and General Staff, whose destruction had been one of our major war aims, should not have been apprehended immediately, but should have been permitted to continue exercising their functions.

The rather lame official explanation was that they were useful in ensuring compliance by the German forces with the surrender terms. It was believed they were co-operating loyally—until it was discovered that they had been shielding Alfred Rosenberg, one of the top Nazi leaders, in their compound. It was this that precipitated their arrest.

We would have been more surprised if we had been told that half a year later German officers in full uniform would still be circulating freely in Hamburg and other cities of the British zone. The British Army showed a kind of chivalry to the defeated foe and was inclined to the attitude that an officer is an officer and should be treated with due respect no matter to what army he belonged. The official British explanation was that it was convenient and efficient to use German Staffs to demobilize the large German Army units that had surrendered during the last days of the war; and that it was expedient to use German-officered labour groups in order to economize British man-power.

I am convinced that there was nothing more sinister than this in the British motives; but the Russians were not convinced. On November 30, 1945, Marshal Zhukov, in a formal statement at a Control Council meeting, made a sensational charge against the British. He claimed to have information that important units of the German Army and Air Force were being trained in the British zone. He said they included:

The German Army Group North, with its field administration and staff;

Two corps groups (Stockhausen and Witthof), each with over 100,000 men;

Five military corps districts;

Twenty-five district and local command posts;

The II Air District headquarters;

Detachments of the 18th Anti-Aircraft Division;

Bomber, fighter and attack squadrons, and close reconnaissance groups;

Over five regiments of communications forces;

Tank regiments;

Military hospitals with over 20,000 beds;

German naval forces (called the Trawler Service) with a
naval staff, patrol formations and flotillas;

1,000,000 soldiers and officers in Schleswig-Holstein,
who were not treated as prisoners of war and were carrying
out military training;

Hungarian detachments of over 12,000 men, organized
into regiments and detachments;

An Esthonian reserve regiment numbering over 3,200
men; and Lithuanian and Latvian detachments totalling
over 21,000 men.

Zhukov said the British were not carrying out the agreed
disarmament and demobilization policies. He added that the
Soviet command considered it imperative to raise the question
of the dispatch of a commission of the Control Council into the
British zone in order to ascertain on the spot the position of the
liquidation and disarmament of the German armed forces.
The Russians clearly entertained the suspicion that the British
were keeping units of the German Army intact for possible
future use against the Soviet Union.

In reply, Montgomery said he was astonished at Zhukov's
statement because it was the first occasion on which one zone
commander had openly challenged the administration of
another. He was also astonished because correspondence on
the subject had passed between the British and Soviet delegations and the matter had been openly discussed in Co-ordinating Committee meetings. He had admitted the existence of
personnel under his command awaiting disbandment. General
Robertson had sent two letters to Zhukov outlining the situation. Neither letter had been acknowledged. The explanations
given in them had not been accepted. They had not been
rejected. They had been ignored.

He explained that the Germans were not classed as prisoners
of war because that would entitle them to higher food rations
than the civilian population (according to the Geneva Con-
vention), and would preclude their doing certain types of
work. They were completely disarmed, and would be dis-

banded as soon as possible, bearing in mind the British need for labour and the agreement on inter-zonal transfers. He admitted there were 99,000 Germans in the Stockhausen area, but said the Witthof area did not exist, and that there were not 1,000,000 but 148,000 men in Schleswig-Holstein.

Montgomery denied that there was an army group headquarters of the German Army. He said the staffs of officers were used purely for administrative purposes and included no operational departments and bore no resemblance to war-time staffs. He denied that there were any air squadrons or groups or any tank detachments. He said it was impossible to repatriate 27,000 Hungarians in the British zone because the Russians would not grant transit facilities through Austria. He charged that Russian liaison officers at his headquarters had been abusing British hospitality by sending back false reports. He was fully satisfied that the British were carrying out the terms of Potsdam, and would accept a commission of inquiry on two conditions: that it visited all four zones with equal freedom of movement; and that it be the first of a series and be followed by others to inquire into various matters.

Zhukov answered that Montgomery's declaration had failed completely to convince him that there were no organized German units or headquarters in his zone. Even if the Germans were disarmed, they could quickly be put on a military footing. He had no reason to suspect Field-Marshal Montgomery of wanting to make war with him; but, as the Soviet Commander-in-Chief, he would like the complete and final disarmament of the Germans—in other words, the fulfilment of the decisions of the Potsdam Conference. He agreed that the commission of inquiry might go into all four zones, but considered the second proposal irrelevant and said subsequent commissions might be formed only as and when required.

General McNarney said he could understand the British need to use Germans for essential work, but was surprised at the British method of economizing troops. He thought it was obvious from Montgomery's statement that he had not carried out one of the essential tasks of Potsdam. But he saw no need for a commission of inquiry, since Montgomery had already admitted the existence of the German units. He suggested referring the matter to the Co-ordinating Committee, where the British could submit arguments and proposals for changing the existing structure.

This was done, and on December 17 General Robertson submitted a plan providing for the complete disbandment of personnel in concentration areas, the German staffs to be used to disband them, by January 31. The British proposed to retain 121,000 Germans in prisoner-of-war cages, 120,000 in "Dienstgruppen" (labour units), and 42,000 naval personnel who were operating under British command in the Baltic and North Seas on a minesweeping job that had been approved by the Control Council. Robertson said this programme involved considerable inconvenience and had been developed to allay suspicions and create confidence, but he did not admit that the British Delegation had violated Potsdam.

General Sokolovsky replied that the British programme, when completed, would certainly clear the air. The maintenance of such units posed a political and economic problem. From the political viewpoint it was bound to appear sinister in the eyes of public opinion. On the economic side German personnel could be used better by disbanding the service units and employing the labour through the competent German authorities.

The air was not cleared, however. Early in May the charge against the British was repeated by Mr. Molotov at the Foreign Ministers' Conference in Paris. The charge was publicized at about the same time by Mr. Walter Lippmann, whose facts were, however, inaccurate. He apparently really believed that the British, behind a "silken curtain", were maintaining a "shadow army" which they were keeping on ice for use against the Russians, if needed. He also believed that both the British and Russians were bent on maintaining the integrity of Prussia, with the idea that by controlling Prussia it would be easy to control Germany. He wrote:

"Prussia has not been decentralized. On the contrary . . . the British and the Russians are more and more committed to promising the Germans a unified and centralized Prussia, dominating a unified and centralized Reich."

This is rather like setting up straw men in order to knock them down because Prussia has been more than decentralized: it has been liquidated. Neither the Russians nor the British nor the Germans themselves have shown any signs of wanting to revive it. Some of the most important parts of this State, which united Germany under its own domination, are in the lands detached from Germany at Potsdam: East Prussia, Silesia, eastern Pomerania. The rest of Prussia is divided between the Soviet and British zones, and has been broken down into its constituent provinces in the Russian zone or shaped up into new smaller entities in the British zone.

In June I went into the British zone for the specific purpose of looking for the "phantom army". I know enough about armies to know that it would be impossible to maintain any large force in an area the size of the British zone without its presence being obvious to a competent observer. If there had been such an army, I would have seen evidences of it. I would have heard about it from the Germans themselves. Of course there wasn't any "silken curtain". American correspondents had been living in the British zone and travelling freely there for months, and they would have spotted any German army very quickly if it had existed.

My trip convinced me that the British demobilization policy was unfortunate, but certainly not sinister. It would have been preferable to disband the 107,000 men in the Dienstgruppen and employ them through the local German labour offices rather than in organized units. Perhaps the British were reluctant to do this because the majority of the men they had retained lived in the Soviet zone, and if they had been sent home, their labour would have been lost to the British zone economy. The British zone was over-populated, but it was short of labour because almost all the refugees flooding in from the east were women and children and old people and disabled men, the Russians and Poles having retained the able-bodied men.

The Dienstgruppen and the German demobilization staffs had undoubtedly encouraged militarism among the Germans to some extent, and had given some of the German officers involved the impression that their military careers were not over, and that they would, indeed, be used in a war against Russia. It was only at the time of my trip that the British, acting under the pressure of the second Russian protest and the Lippmann articles, began requiring German officers to remove their rank insignia, stop calling themselves by their rank titles, and stop saluting each other.

The 325 separate Dienstgruppen, averaging 300 to 400 men each, were in no sense military cadres. There was no German

173

chain of command integrating the several groups. The men were unarmed and did no military training. Nor did the high general staff officers whom the British kept in a camp in Belgium constitute a basis for reconstituting the general staff. They were being kept prisoners awaiting their disposition at the completion of the Nuernberg trial. They were treated as prisoners of war, and nothing was done to give them the impression that they would one day resume their careers as staff officers.

Molotov's charge was made in answer to Byrnes' proposal for a twenty-five-year treaty to keep Germany disarmed and demilitarized. Molotov suggested that it would be more useful to complete the demilitarization of Germany in the west. To overcome this objection, Byrnes proposed a four-power commission to investigate the progress of disarmament and demilitarization in the four zones. The proposal was accepted. The commission never started its work, however, because the Russians would not agree that it should investigate economic as well as military disarmament. The British and Americans wanted to broaden the scope of the investigation in this way because they had information that specialized war materials were being produced in the Soviet zone.

There can be little doubt that these reports were based on fact. I was reliably told that 75 per cent of the production of the Zeiss optical plant at Jena was for military purposes. A part of the Schweinfurt ball-bearing plant, which was given to Russia as reparations, was set up again in the Soviet zone. Experimental work on V-weapons (rockets) was going on in the zone.

One American correspondent once had an opportunity to talk with a German in Leipzig who told him about war production that was going on in certain plants. A month later this correspondent returned to the Soviet zone, and this same German acted as a guide. In the presence of Russian officers, he denied that there was any war production in any part of the zone, extending his denial specifically to the plants he had previously mentioned. At the end of the day he took advantage of a momentary absence of the Russian officers to draw the American correspondent aside.

"Didn't I have a talk with you in Leipzig about a month ago?" the German asked. The correspondent said he remembered the talk.

"Well," said the German, "nothing has changed."

In spite of all this, I do not believe the Russians were trying to reconstitute the German war potential in their zone. What they were trying to do was to catch up in the technical development of strategic weapons. In certain cases they found it more convenient to do this in Germany than to transport the facilities to Russia. In other cases they took German scientists, like Manfred von Ardenne, the inventor of the electron-microscope and builder of the first cyclotron in Germany, and Dr. Gustav Hertz, Nobel prize-winner in Physics, to Russia to work on atom-bomb development. Such men were given the best working and living conditions possible.

It should be added that the Americans were not behindhand in picking the brains of German scientists. If the Americans were indignant at the Russian removals of machinery from what was to be the United States sector of Berlin, the Russians were equally put out when they discovered the Americans had made away with most of the faculty of the Science Departments of Halle, Leipzig and Jena universities and with top technicians from the Zeiss optical works, the Buna artificial rubber factory and the Leuna synthetic-fuel plant.

Lippmann's mistake was one of degree and emphasis rather than of kind. He was right in seeing a contest in progress between the Russians and the British for the control of Germany. (The Americans and French are also involved in the contest, incidentally.) He was wrong in believing it had gone so far that the Allies were rebuilding the Germans' military and economic strength to be used against each other. It is true that all the Allies have been anxious to make use of German technical knowledge to speed the development of their own research in the field of nightmarish weapons. That is a contest which goes far beyond the German problem. In Germany the struggle has been almost entirely in the ideological arena.

That is not to say that this struggle is not inherently dangerous; it is merely to put it in its proper perspective. An alarmist and hysterical interpretation of what is going on in Germany will only make a settlement more difficult. And a German settlement is one of the basic prerequisites of peace in Europe. What such a settlement might be, I shall endeavour to show in my next and final chapter.

XII

A POSSIBLE GERMAN SETTLEMENT

THE ideological contest between Russia and the west, which at the present time characterizes the struggle between the two world-power groups, is not limited to Germany. It embraces the great globe itself. Germany is but one of several vital, strategic areas in the borderland between east and west. The use of geographical terms in this connection is for convenience. It is not literally accurate, since the borderland stretches from Scandinavia in a wide arc through central Europe, the Middle East and all the way round to Manchuria and Korea.

In Europe, the nursery of our civilization, Germany is the most important arena of conflict because of its central position, its large population, its resources and its great industrial potential. What has been happening in Germany is naturally conditioned by policies as they are shaped in Washington and Moscow, in London and Paris, and by the relations between the Great Powers as they develop in international conferences. These policies and relations are in turn affected by what happens in Germany, where they are constantly being tested.

A German settlement obviously cannot be considered *in vacuo*, but only as it will affect and be affected by these relations between the Powers. Further, it cannot be expected that a good German settlement will remove all causes of friction and conflict between the Powers. Many of these causes are to be found outside Germany; they have their roots in differing philosophies of government and economics as well as in national rivalries. They involve such truly fundamental questions as these: Can a capitalist America and a socialist Russia live peacefully in the same world? Does the Soviet Union aim at a world revolution, or is it an aggressively expanding national State, or is it merely interested in its own security? Will a major depression in this country cause the United States to become, as the Russians seem to fear, an aggressive, militaristic, imperialist force? I do not believe there are any simple answers to these questions. They go beyond the scope of this book, and I have touched on them merely to show that the very existence of these burning questions profoundly affects the atmosphere in which the problem of Germany is being considered.

A German settlement will be a good one if it minimizes instead of intensifying the explosive possibilities of the world conflict of power and ideologies. Ideally such a settlement should make it impossible for Germany to be a source of disputes that could lead to war. Germany should be "neutralized" so that neither side need fear that the German war potential will be used against it by the other side. The Germans themselves should not be placed in a position where they will be tempted to play off one side against the other.

Before outlining my ideas of what the details of such a settlement should be, I believe it is worth while to summarize what may be called the factual bases on which a settlement will have to be made. In other words, what does it all add up to—everything that has been happening in Germany in the last two years?

We find that Germany is wrecked: it is a physical and moral wilderness. A country whose civilization had achieved a high technical development is now reduced to primitive conditions. A population of some 70,000,000 is existing near the starvation level, is living in ruins, is unable to satisfy its simplest needs. Production has not been restored even to the level advocated by those who favour dealing most harshly with the German people. This situation is primarily the result of the war, but it has been perpetuated and aggravated by the division of Germany into economically unviable units and by a failure to agree on policies for its revival.

Morally, Germany is a wilderness for a number of reasons. I believe the German mind is sick, and that fact is necessary to an understanding of Hitlerism. Furthermore, the best German elements have been killed off by the Nazis. But again Allied policies or lack of policy have aggravated the situation. The Allies have so far failed to show the Germans a possible way. The word democracy is used freely, but the Germans have not been told what democracy can mean for them in concrete terms. They have not been told how they can play a constructive rôle in the world of to-morrow, and failing this they are likely to think in non-constructive terms. I am not saying that it would be enough to give the Germans prosperity for them to throw off all their faults and be "good". What I am

177

saying is that the truly miserable conditions in Germany to-day are bound to foster hate and bitterness, to make the Germans truly unregenerate, to frustrate any efforts at re-education and any attempts to encourage the growth of democracy.

Against this background, the occupation Powers have been trying to carry out the Potsdam programme for preventing Germany from ever again being able to threaten the peace of the world. Demilitarization has been completed for all practical purposes. The German Army has been disbanded, the main fortifications demolished, stocks of arms blown up or dumped in the sea, submarines scuttled and their pens sealed up, war factories dismantled or destroyed. As a military Power, Germany does not exist at the present time.

Politically, the bases of decentralization have been laid. The Prussian State has been liquidated. A number of smaller States and city-States have been incorporated into larger administrative units. There are now in the several zones of Germany a total of just under twenty medium-sized States and provinces that could form the basis for a federal republic. The liquidation of the large feudal estates and the programme for breaking up cartels and monopolies are destroying the economic power bases of past Germany aggression.

The progress in denazification has been less encouraging. The heart of this problem is the need for finding people to take the place of the Nazis, who in the main monopolized all the positions of influence and power in administration, industry and business. Standards are hard to set because Party affiliation is not a reliable yardstick. All Nazis were not "bad" and all non-Nazis were not "good". One is dealing not with blacks and whites, but with different shades of grey, and the millions of people involved magnify the task to be accomplished to unmanageable proportions. The real need is to develop positively democratic forces, thereby taking the emphasis off the negative aspects of denazification.

As I have repeatedly emphasized, all these problems are enormously complicated by the struggle among the victors for the body and soul of Germany. In this struggle it may be said that Russia has lost the first round. The Soviets have failed to gain the political allegiance of the Germans. Prophets who predicted that Germany would go Communist if it lost the war have been proved wrong. In Berlin, in Hamburg, in Frankfurt and in the Ruhr, even in Dresden and Leipzig in the

Russian zone, the Communists have done considerably less well than in the last of the pre-Hitler elections.

It might have been expected that the levelling influence of the war, which by destroying property values and relationships turned Germany into a nation of dispossessed, would have created favourable conditions for Communism. Furthermore, there was the general misery, with almost the entire population hungry, with millions homeless, with so many opportunities for gainful employment cut off, and with monetary inflation developing in an alarming manner. Yet the Germans did not, in this situation, choose Communism. One reason may have been that, despite their lack of a long democratic tradition, many of them had, under Nazism, developed a healthy dislike for absolute dictatorship; there were few who wanted to substitute a Communist dictatorship for the Nazi one.

I have outlined how the Russian actions and policies themselves contributed to the anti-Communist trend. The manner and extent of Russian reparations removals were the largest single factor. If many Germans were realistic enough to place the blame for their miseries where it belonged, on Hitler and his war, they could see these miseries being indefinitely prolonged by Russian reparations exactions. Every time the Russians dismantled a factory they took jobs away from its workers, and these workers were most likely lost to the Communist cause. If the workers were highly skilled, the Russians might take them along, too, but that did not increase Soviet popularity with the Germans.

The Russians have also lost the first round in Germany, in that they are not getting the reparations they had counted on from western Germany. It was their refusal to agree to use the resources of all German zones for the benefit of the whole country and to work out a common import-export plan that precipitated Clay's suspension of reparations removals from the American zone. The British, too, have been holding back on the dismantling of reparations plants, waiting to see if the other Potsdam provisions would be put into practice.

In their own zone the Russians found that their removals were uneconomical. The plants they removed deteriorated so much while being dismantled and transported and reassembled that it would have been better to have left them in Germany and taken the produce. Since the middle of 1946 they have actually been taking most of their reparations in the form of current production, but they have taken so much out that the whole economy of the zone is in danger of complete disruption.

It looks as though the Soviet policy, if it can be called a policy, of taking as much as possible as quickly as possible will prove to have been short-sighted from their own point of view, and that soon there will not be so much to take. In other words, if they do not actually succeed in killing the goose that lays the golden eggs, they are at any rate, by neglecting and starving it, making it a very sick goose, that won't be laying nearly as many of those proverbial eggs.

The political setbacks suffered by the Russians are hardly just grounds for complacence on the part of Americans. We may be winning on points in Germany, but we would gain nothing by a knock-out. The struggle that is going on between us and the Russians is a fact; and we would not be free to retire from it even if we wished to do so. But our present advantage can best be used to help us reach a settlement with the Russians.

I do not believe this struggle is as imminently dangerous as one might conclude from reading the scare headlines in many American papers. In so far as it is played out on the ideological field, this contest is not entirely harmful. If Americans really believe in the principles of their democracy, they should be willing to support these principles in all parts of the world.

Therefore our representatives in Germany are right in doing all they can to uphold the American conception of democracy as opposed to the Russian concept. In this early post-war period the Germans have shown that they incline to favour the Western type of democracy. This may not always be so. For instance, it would almost certainly be a mistake for Americans to try to go beyond supporting the forms of democracy as we know them by attempting to re-establish in Germany anything like the kind of capitalism we have in the United States. Germany can no longer afford the luxury of our style of capitalism, and the Germans know it.

The British, whose own situation is similar, differing only in degree from that of the Germans, have themselves decided that they must turn away from capitalism. They have had the sense to see that by supporting socialism in Germany they will be doing not only the economically correct thing, but also the best thing politically. They will be stealing the thunder of the Russians. The best way to combat communism in Europe to-day is with socialism.

Hence the bold British decision to go ahead with preparations for nationalizing such key industries in Germany as coal and steel, chemicals and electrical engineering. These industries cannot be turned over to the German Government now, because there is no German Government; so the British proposed to hold them in trust for the German people. There is, of course, a potential danger in this proceeding, as such industries could be potent weapons in the hands of some future German Government. It all depends on what kind of a German Government we get. And the British believe that the way to get the right kind of German Government is to give the German democrats a fair chance. This can only be done by creating the most favourable economic conditions possible.

This British policy has clashed with the American de-cartelization programme, and the differences between the two conceptions were brought to the fore after the agreement to unify the two zones economically. The British have been forced to agree to such a reduction in the size of plants that no single one shall employ more than 10,000 workers. The immediate consequences will not be very great, but there is no doubt that this ceiling, if maintained, will greatly impede any attempts at restoring efficient production.

I have said that the struggle that is going on between Russia and the West is one from which we cannot retire. That does not mean it is one that can never be composed. Obviously some *modus vivendi* with the Russians must be found, must be worked out in the course of the next five, ten, fifteen years if the struggle is not to end in war. The Nazis, right up until the last years of the war, placed their hopes on just such a conflict between Russia and the Western democracies. Undoubtedly there are still Germans who see some hope of salvation in this struggle. Fortunately there are other Germans who realize the stupidity of such a policy. For in the long run, if a war results, Germany would almost certainly be a battlefield, and in that event its sufferings would be infinitely greater than its recent and present ones. Even in the short run, the Germans will be the chief losers from an aggravation of the East–West conflict.

In order to understand this one must try to imagine what would happen if the Allies came to the point where they all recognized that they could not agree what to do with Germany. The Russians would then presumably decide to abandon any idea of exercising any influence or control in western Germany; while the Western Allies would make a similar abdication with respect to eastern Germany. Sooner or later the experiment in quadripartite government would be abandoned, which would mean that the Americans, the British and the French would have no more reason to stay in Berlin. They would eventually leave the capital, which would no longer be a capital except for the Soviet zone. The line through the centre of Germany would become a frontier fixed for an indefinite period.

This is a compelling reason for urgency in reaching a settlement. For in the absence of agreement the East–West division of Germany tends to sharpen. This division has nothing to do with a healthy decentralization. What is happening is an integration of eastern Germany with the Soviet economy. On the other side, the integration of western Germany with the economy of western Europe has not gone so far, but the trend is there. The longer these trends are continued, the harder will it become to reintegrate the whole German economy in such a way that it can take its proper place in the general European economy. There could be little profit to the Germans in such a splitting of their country, and they know it. From the global point of view, it would mean the beginning of the replacement of the borderland area between the two worlds by firm and fixed frontiers.

The Germans themselves may be able to do something to prevent this consummation, one that is not "devoutly to be wished". They could try to form a bridge between East and West. In order to do this they would have to convince all the Allies that they do not intend to be utilized by one side against the other. And the Western Allies would have to find some way —and there is no easy way—of convincing the Russians that a victory for the Western type of democracy in Germany will not mean a Germany that will be used by the West against Russia.

In this connection the example of Czechoslovakia is instructive. The experience of this small nation is the most hopeful—one of the few hopeful elements in the European situation. Czechoslovakia is in the process of becoming a socialist State without abandoning the forms of democracy.

It has been able to maintain friendly relations with Russia without being dominated by Russia, without closing its door to cultural influences from the West or to trade and commerce with the West (although American reluctance to extend credits may yet force the Czechs to orient their economy to the East). The Communists are the largest single party in Czechoslovakia, but they are not in a majority, and so far have preferred to co-operate with the other parties rather than seize power and establish a Soviet State. A sincere democrat and non-Communist like Mr. Mazaryk appears convinced that the Communist co-operation is loyal. All this might be changed by a further deterioration of relations between Russia and the United States. Asked recently what would happen to Czechoslovakia's uranium in the event of war, Mazaryk quipped that he did not think it would go to New Zealand. To date, however, Czechoslovakia has achieved remarkable success in making itself a bridge between East and West.

For Germany to do the same thing—to become a truly neutral country, trusted by both major parties—would be an infinitely more difficult task. For one thing, Germany is so much bigger, potentially more powerful, that its failure to observe true neutrality, its defection to one side or the other, would have much graver consequences. Then the Russians are less inclined to trust the Germans than their Slavic brothers in Czechoslovakia. The Germans themselves have shown less evidence than the Czechs of the kind of political astuteness they need if they are to adopt such a rôle.

I do not suggest that we should count on the ability of the Germans to build this "bridge". What I propose is a settlement that would make it easier for them to do it, but would at the same time provide reliable guarantees against a resurgence of German military power, and would thus reduce the Allies' causes for concern to a minimum. I believe this should be done through controls, and that the controls should be simple to administer. There should be as few opportunities as possible for disagreement among the Allies about interpretation and implementation of the terms to be imposed on Germany. We should learn from the example of Potsdam, which made necessary a government of Germany by negotiation.

The first thing to do is to draw up a list of prohibitions. It might read something like this. Germany may not have an army, an air force or a navy. Germany may not engage in

183

atomic research. Germany may not construct submarines or warships of any kind. Germany may not build aircraft or tanks. Germany may not produce arms or ammunition. This list is not necessarily exhaustive; the idea is that whatever is useful for war and only for war should be outlawed. Germany would engage itself in the peace treaty to abide by these prohibitions, and to accept Allied control commissions, with complete freedom of investigation, for a period of, say, twenty-five years, the arrangement to be renewable at the end of that period if any of the Allies concerned considered it necessary. A limited number of small-arms for the German civil police could be permitted, but they could not be produced in Germany.

The advantage of such a plan is that it could easily be enforced. Teams of Allied experts, with freedom to investigate any German factory, could quickly detect a violation of the terms. It takes years to build up an aircraft or submarine industry to the point where one single plane or submarine can be produced. Any violation could be spotted in the early stages. It might be argued that after the last war Germany rearmed secretly. This is not true: it was generally known that Germany was violating the Versailles Treaty and rearming, but nothing was done about it. This time, qualified inspectors must watch for any signs that the Germans are producing arms or are preparing to convert peace factories to war production. For instance, periodic checks on automobile and tractor factories would ascertain whether there was any attempt to convert them to production of aircraft or tanks, and similar checks on shipyards would guard against the construction of submarines or surface warships. A prohibition on the construction of merchant vessels would then be unnecessary. Such ships are needed to help handle Germany's foreign trade and to provide employment for the workers in cities like Hamburg and Bremen.

Violations of the agreement would be reported at once to the central control commission in Berlin, which would be required to take immediate steps to end the violation. Failure to do so would result in dismantling of the factories concerned. Any signs that Germany's armed forces were being reconstituted could be dealt with in similar fashion. It takes years to form and train an army from scratch. After the first war, Germany was left with an army of 100,000 men, which really

184

served as an officers' training-school and a cadre for later quick expansion. Even this expansion was not done secretly. All the former Allies knew about it; but nothing was done about it. The important thing is to set up a mechanism whereby violations will automatically be dealt with, and will not have to be the subject for diplomatic negotiations.

Every time Hitler violated the Versailles Treaty, announcing to the world that he was doing so, there were consultations between the former Allied Governments, but there was no easy mechanism with which to block the violation. Under the scheme proposed here Germany could never become powerful enough to face the Allies with an important *fait accompli*, because any attempts at rearming would be detected immediately and nipped in the bud. There would not be the same possibilities of quadripartite disagreement as now exist, because all that would be necessary would be to agree on the facts of whether a certain forbidden product was being manufactured. Such facts would be easily ascertainable.

The problem would be further simplified by eliminating prohibitions and restrictions on a long list of products that serve a war economy indirectly. Thus, ball-bearings, steel, machine tools, synthetic rubber, synthetic gasoline, merchant ships, etc., are all very important to a war economy. But they have no military value as long as airplanes, tanks, guns, shells, rifles, bullets, and a number of other things are not being produced. On the other hand, ball-bearings, steel, machine-tools, etc., are also vital to a peace economy. It would be part of the duties of the Allied commissions to find out where every ton of steel and every ball-bearing went. They could do this without interfering in the German productive process. A certain steel factory would be required to open its books to the commission and account for its production. So and so many tons were exported; so and so many went to such and such German plants. The commission would then carry out spot-checks to make sure that this was what was actually happening to the steel. In cases where some special suspicion had arisen a more thorough check would have to be carried out. There is no doubt that attempts to circumvent such a control system could not long go undetected.

The same objection might be raised that Mr. Lilienthal foresaw against an inspection scheme in connection with atomic energy—namely, that a policing job of this kind is uninteresting, and it would be difficult to find qualified people who would devote their time to it. Therefore lack of interest on the part of those enforcing the scheme would cause it to bog down.

These objections would not apply here, because the personnel requirements of a plan for enforcing German disarmament would be much more modest than those of any plan for control of atomic production on a world-wide basis. Furthermore, the same degree of scientific and technical excellence would not be required. By reducing the prohibitions to a short list of key products, the task is greatly simplified. Officers competent to rule on whether the prohibitions I have listed were being violated exist in every regular army. Indeed, one advantage of the plan is that it provides a substitute for mass-occupation armies. The United States, for instance, will be unwilling to keep a large army in Germany for very many years; but it will always be able and ready to supply enough officers and men to take part in a simple control scheme of this nature.

The plan presupposes the abolition of the occupation zones. As long as this division is maintained, Germany can never be treated as an economic unit. Even if it were possible to reach an agreement in principle, it would be impossible in practice to prevent local military forces from interfering with representatives of the German Government. This is strongly indicated by experience in Germany to date. In the Soviet zone there are central administrative agencies for industry, transportation, trade, etc. The German heads of these agencies, no matter whether they are Communists or not, complain that they cannot perform the tasks set them by the Soviet High Command because of the interference of local Red Army commanders in the provinces. In the American zone, the minister presidents of the States have made similar complaints of interference with their subordinates by troops commanders or local military government officials. Extend this situation to the national plane, and the complications multiply. It would be very difficult, for instance, for the Americans and British to devise any system whereby economic unity would not merely mean a free flow of goods from the West into the Soviet zone, whence they would be siphoned off into Russia. This is what actually happened in Austria, with the result that economic unity rapidly became a farce.

There is another very strong argument against continuing the division of Germany into zones. Their existence encourages mutual criticism by the Allies of each other's occupation policies, and even encourages German groups and parties to criticize individual Allies, thus joining in the general propaganda war. For instance, a Communist leader attacks the Western Allies for failing to denazify; or a Social Democrat attacks the Russians for the removal of factory equipment. I would propose that the Allied Control Authority be kept in Berlin, and that the German Government, when it is formed, be made responsible to the Control Council for certain specific things. Then there could be subsidiary control commissions in the capitals of each of the States or provinces. All these commissions would include representatives of each of the four occupation Powers. Thus there would be joint responsibility throughout Germany, and the chances for invidious comparisons would be greatly reduced.

What should be the powers and functions of the Allied control forces? Eventually I believe they should be reduced to ensuring the continuation of German disarmament, as outlined above. In the first few years after the peace treaty and the formation of a German Government they might have to continue certain other functions, but these should be specifically defined in line with a joint policy to be agreed during the peace negotiations. There might still be a need for denazification after the signing of the treaty. If so, the German Government should be charged with setting up a Ministry of Denazification and proposing a plan for completion of the denazification programme. It would report to the Allied Control Council, and would be disbanded as soon as the Allies were unanimously agreed that it had satisfactorily fulfilled its mission.

Education is a field in which the Allies might properly continue to take an interest for some time to come. It will admittedly be difficult for them to agree on what should be taught in German schools. Yet this is so fundamental a problem that I believe agreement on an educational policy for Germany should form an important part of the peace negotiations. Once such a policy had been developed, it would be up to the German Ministry of Education to carry it out, but in the initial period it would be responsible to the Allied Control Council.

The Control Council would likewise supervise the fulfilment by Germany of its reparations obligations. These must naturally be fixed in the peace treaty. Both a total figure and a schedule by years should be set. This schedule would be subject to revision in the light of experience and changing circumstances. Reparations should be light during the time necessary to permit the recovery of Germany's productive apparatus. The Germans would be given both hope and encouragement to work harder by knowing that once this obligation had been fulfilled, they would have done their war penance and could go about raising their own living standards. The system of simple controls over war production that I have proposed would permit a German peace production high enough to provide the Russians and other claimant nations with substantial reparations over a period of years, and this should in turn make it easier to reach an agreement with the Russians on other aspects of the peace settlement.

For many years after the signing of the peace treaty it will be necessary to keep some military force in Germany (the control commissions would not represent any real armed power). Since the occupation zones and armies would be abolished, I would propose a kind of international constabulary—mobile units of tanks, armoured cars, jeeps and motor cycles, and perhaps some air squadrons. The main purpose of this constabulary would be to show the Germans that the Allied commissions are backed by force, and are to be taken seriously. The short-lived Allied disarmament commissions established after the First World War failed partly because they were not backed by military force on the spot.

This constabulary would have no right to interfere with the Germany economy or with the private lives of individual Germans. Its main duty would be to show itself, to move about the country, to serve as a reminder to the Germans that their obligations under the peace treaty are not to be taken lightly. As far as possible, American, Russian, British and French units should be integrated, even in small units. This would serve the joint purpose of giving nationals of the four countries a chance to know each other better as comrades in arms, and of rendering impossible unilateral actions by armed forces of individual countries. If the Allies cannot reach agreement to integrate their forces in this fashion, it should at any rate be specified that no armed unit has any jurisdiction over or right

188

to interference in the administration of the area in which it happens to be stationed. The period of this form of semi-occupation would not be set in advance; its termination would be agreed upon in taking account of the conduct of the German Government and population.

The German Government should not have the right to conclude any alliances or separate treaties or political arrangements with any country. The date for Germany's admission to the United Nations would naturally depend on the confidence inspired by the German Government.

I fully agree with Mr. Byrnes' contention that the provisional German–Polish boundary should not be final. In particular it takes too much agricultural land away from the Germans. It would be pointless to try to suggest an exact boundary, as this will have to be a negotiated compromise, and no doubt, as in the case of Trieste, no solution satisfactory to all sides can be reached. However, a reasonable compromise might be to let Poland keep East Prussia (apart from what the Russians have taken), Danzig, and Upper Silesia (the Gleiwitz–Ratibor–Oppeln triangle), and return to Germany Lower Silesia (including Breslau), Stettin, and those parts of Brandenburg and Pomerania extending to the pre-1939 frontier, but not including the corridor.

It may be impossible to get the Russians to agree to this revision. However, they might be willing to do so in return for the retention of the Ruhr and Rhineland in Germany and agreement to their reparations demands. I do not mean to say that I regard inclusion of the Ruhr and Rhineland merely as a bargaining asset to be conceded to the Russians. I believe it is important for other reasons as well. On the face of it there is considerable merit in the French proposal to take them away from Germany altogether and form a small internationalized State. This idea is concurred in by many influential Americans —for instance, Mr. John Foster Dulles, who favours using the industry of the Ruhr as the economic keystone of a western European bloc. I do not blame the Russians for their suspicion of the motives behind such a scheme. The idea is to oppose presumed Russian expansionism with a powerful economic bloc in the West. By its inclusion of the industrial area in western Germany, this bloc would obviously represent a powerful war potential.

Proponents of this plan often say: "Detach the Rhineland,

and then you can safely unify the rest of Germany." Or: "Give us the Ruhr and Rhine, and the Russians can have the rest." I have said that one of the objects of a lasting German settlement must be that it should give as few grounds as possible to one side to fear that Germany's war potential would be used against it by the other. This plan does not meet that criterion. An internationalized Ruhr, in which the Russians would have one voice, but could always be outvoted, would give them no security. What would happen would be that the Russians would be put in the position of being able to mobilize German irredentist sentiment against the West, and lead a crusade for getting this territory back in Germany. They would have the German people 100 per cent. behind them. It would be far better to exercise joint four-Power control over the industry of the Ruhr within the framework of a security scheme such as I have proposed above. The task of checking on German production would be made simpler by the fact that most of the important industry is concentrated in the Ruhr–Rhineland region. The commission charged with supervision of this region would naturally have to be much larger, and would have to exercise greater vigilance than those in the rest of Germany.

Before a peace treaty is signed a German Government will have to be formed, and before that is done a constitution will have to be written. The United States should insist that this constitution guarantees the fundamental democratic liberties: a fair electoral system, freedom of speech and of the Press, a bill of rights. However, once this has been done, the United States should not stand in the way of any desire on the part of the German people to adopt a socialist economic system.

The proposals I have outlined in this chapter are the main elements of what I conceive to be a reasonable settlement of the German problem. I believe it is also a possible settlement. Naturally the actual peace settlement, assuming there is one, will have to be a compromise, and I am not so optimistic as to expect that it will look like this in detail. However, I do believe acceptance of the main principles upon which I have based this proposal is essential. These are: a simple plan of inspection and control to guard against German rearmament; encouragement to German industry to produce as much as possible for peaceful purposes, in order to make possible a rapid payment

190

of reparations and to raise living standards in Germany and in Europe; a politically decentralized but unified Germany including the Ruhr and Rhineland and a part of the territories now under Polish administration; abolition of the occupation zones and armies, and their replacement by control commissions and small security forces; rejection of any proposals that encourage one group of Allies to use Germany against the other, or encourage the Germans to exploit differences between the Allies.

While the statesmen negotiate, the Allied Control Authority in Berlin will continue to mark time. Conditions in Germany will become worse rather than better, and will exert a depressing effect on conditions in the surrounding European countries. The Foreign Ministers are now turning more and more of their attention to Germany. It would be too much to hope for a quick solution to the many big problems involved. Yet the longer a settlement is postponed, the more difficult will its achievement become.

A peace treaty for Germany would not, of course, by itself bring harmony and good will to the world. A good treaty would, however, bring Europe greater prosperity, and prosperity promotes peace. It would improve the international atmosphere and help give the nations a breathing spell. That breathing spell is needed if the foundations for an international community, some form of world federation, are ever to be laid. Remote as that goal must seem to-day, it is one toward which the world must strive if it is to avoid committing suicide in a nightmarish atomic-bacteriological war. I do not believe such a war is likely in the next ten or fifteen years. We shall have a period of grace. But this time must be used wisely; it is precious and must not be squandered.

In Germany, however discouraging the outlook may become, there may never be a time when the statesmen will say: "We have failed: we must face it." One must hope devoutly that there will never be such a time. But there is a tendency, in the absence of agreement, for the decision to go by default. Lack of agreement becomes as harmful as a bad agreement. It strengthens the trend toward two Germanies, two Europes, two worlds; two worlds armed against each other and facing each other with mounting hostility.